The NetWare 286 Manual Maker

The NetWare 286 Manual Maker

CHRISTINE MILLIGAN

The Complete Kit for Creating Customized NetWare 286 Manuals

M&T Books
A Division of M&T Publishing, Inc.
501 Galveston Drive
Redwood City, CA 94063

© 1990 by M&T Publishing, Inc.

Printed in the United States of America

All rights reserved. No part of this book may be reproduced or transmitted in any form or by any means, electronic or mechanical, including photocopying, recording, or by any information storage and retrieval system, without prior written permission from the Publisher. Contact the Publisher for information on foreign rights.

Limits of Liability and Disclaimer of Warranty
The Author and Publisher of this book have used their best efforts in preparing this book and the programs contained in it. These efforts include the development, research, and testing of the theories and programs to determine their effectiveness.

The Author and Publisher make no warranty of any kind, expressed or implied, with regard to these programs or the documentation contained in this book. The Author and Publisher shall not be liable in any event for incidental or consequential damages in connection with, or arising out of, the furnishing, performance, or use of these programs.

Library of Congress Cataloging in Publication Data

Milligan, Christine
    The NetWare 286 Manual Maker: the complete kit for creating customized NetWare 286 manuals / Christine Milligan

ISBN 1-55851-119-9 (book/disk)
1. NetWare (Computer operating system) 2. Electronic data processing documentation I. title

QA76.76.063M565 1990
005.7'1369--dc20
                                                                                                      90-19666
                                                                                                           CIP

93 92 91 90   4 3 2 1

All products, names, and services are trademarks or registered trademarks of their respective companies.

Editor: Tova F. Fliegel   **Cover Design**: Lauren Smith Designs

Contents

WHY THIS BOOK IS FOR YOU 1

INTRODUCTION: HOW TO USE MANUAL MAKER 3
Purposes of the Manual Maker 4
The Manual Maker Format 5
Backing Up the Master Files 7
What You Can Create with the Manual Maker 8
Using the Manual Maker: A Suggested Approach 9
WordPerfect and ASCII Formats 11
Information for WordPerfect Users 12
Information for ASCII Users 16

CHAPTER 1: INTRODUCTION TO NETWORKING AND NETWARE 19
What is a Network? 22
Essential Network Components 23
Network Peripherals 26
A Description of Our Network 27
Conclusion 28

**CHAPTER 2: GETTING ON AND OFF THE NETWORK,
LOGGING IN AND OUT** 29
Why You Have to Log In 31
How to Log In 32
What You See After You Log In 38

THE NETWARE 286 MANUAL MAKER

Batch Files and Login Scripts 39
A Basic Display 40
Custom Menus 42
Logging In to More than One Server at a Time 53
How to Change Your Password 54
Logging Out 56
Conclusion 57

CHAPTER 3: NETWORK RESTRICTIONS 59
Login Restrictions 62
Disk Restrictions 68
Conclusion 73

HOW TO USE CHAPTERS 4 AND 5 75

CHAPTER 4: WORKING WITH DIRECTORIES AND FILES
(FILES UTILITIES VERSION) 77
Directory Structures 80
A Sample Directory Structure 81
Directory Paths 82
NetWare Security 83
Approaches to NetWare Security 83
Viewing Your Effective Rights Throughout the Directory Tree 91
Checking Your Effective Rights for Individual Directories 96
Viewing Your Effective Rights Throughout the Directory Tree 99
Checking Your Effective Rights for Individual Directories 104
How Your Effective Rights Were Determined 105
Security Attributes 108
Moving Up and Down the Directory Tree 109
Drive Mappings 110
Search Drive Mappings 113
Looking at Files 115
Copying Files 117

CONTENTS

Deleting and Renaming Files 119
Backing Up and Restoring Files 120
Salvaging Files 121
Printing Files 122
Working with Directories 125
Ideas for Creating Your Own Directory Structures 126
Creating a Directory 128
Setting Up Drive Mappings 129
Saving Mappings in Login Scripts 130
Setting Security 132
Conclusion 136

CHAPTER 5: WORKING WITH DIRECTORIES AND FILES
(MENU UTILITIES VERSION) 139

Directory Structures 142
A Sample Directory Structure 143
Directory Paths 144
Exploring the Directory Tree 145
Drive Mappings 146
Search Drive Mappings 147
Your Effective Rights 156
How Your Effective Rights Were Determined 161
Security Attributes 162
Looking at Files 163
Copying Files 164
Deleting and Renaming Files 165
Backing Up and Restoring Files 166
Printing Files 167
Working with Directories 169
Ideas for Creating Your Own Directory Structure 171
Setting Up Drive Mappings 173
Saving Mappings in Login Scripts 174
Setting Security 175
Conclusion 179

THE NETWARE 286 MANUAL MAKER

CHAPTER 6: COMMAND LINE UTILITIES REFERENCE 181
Deciding What Utilities to Include 183
Making a Master List of Users' Rights 186
Utilities Reference 187

CHAPTER 7: MENU UTILITIES REFERENCE 243
Deciding What Tasks to Include 245
Making a Master List of Users' Rights 248
Menu Utilities Reference 249

CHAPTER 8: INSTRUCTIONS FOR FINAL FORMATTING 329
Formatting WordPerfect Files 331
Formatting Other Types of Files 337

Why The NetWare 286 Manual Maker is for You

If you need to write documentation or train users, *The NetWare 286 Manual Maker* is for you! It consists of generic end-user documentation which can easily be modified to suit your network setup, administration philosophy and policies, and users' expertise. Just delete the material you don't want; modify the fill-in-the-blank templates; and add any material that's specific to your installation. You'll have clear, concise, customized documentation in a matter of days instead of months.

System supervisors can create user-specific documentation. It's easy to delete utilities you don't want users to know about; document how your network is set up; and explain the specific menus, login scripts, and batch files you use on your network.

Dealers and consultants can create custom end-user documentation for their customers, then keep a copy on file for their own use. If the network setup or the customers' needs change, modifying the documentation accordingly is a snap. (Just think what this could do to increase your sales and decrease your support burden!)

End-users benefit from documentation and training that is precisely tailored to their needs. No more searching through pages and pages of irrelevant information, or scrawling notes in margins. The Manual Maker eliminates all of that. Users get a small manual which contains exactly the information that they need to be productive on the network immediately.

No matter who you are, *The NetWare 286 Manual Maker* can save you time, money, and frustration. It's an invaluable tool that will pay for itself in a matter of hours.

INTRODUCTION

How to Use The NetWare 286 Manual Maker

Instructions for Supervisors

This chapter provides an overall explanation of how to use *The NetWare 286 Manual Maker*. It also explains some details you should understand before you begin working with the Manual Maker.

HOW TO USE THE NETWARE 286 MANUAL MAKER

Purposes of the Manual Maker

The NetWare 286 Manual Maker has several purposes.

Create customized user manuals. The main purpose of the Manual Maker is to help you create user manuals that are tailored to your network setup, philosophy of administering the network, and users' expertise.

The Manual Maker consists mainly of boilerplate documents that you can modify to create your user manuals. Hard copy of the boilerplates forms the bulk of this book; soft copy is provided on the diskettes that accompany this book. The Manual Maker also contains information that helps you to modify the boilerplate text, teach users, and set up their network environments.

Help you teach users. You can use the Manual Maker to create training materials or develop course outlines. Because of this, the Manual Maker contains some ideas for teaching and training users in a classroom setting.

Give tips and tricks. Many times, what you teach users depends on how you have set up the network environment they work in. The Manual Maker also provides miscellaneous tips and tricks on setting up the network environments.

INTRODUCTION

The Manual Maker Format

The Manual Maker consists of two types of text:

Boilerplate text. This is the actual text that you can modify and include in your customized user manuals.

Ideas and information. This text is intended only for you as supervisor, and is not intended to be included in your user manuals.

The ideas and in formation intended only for you as supervisor are presented in three forms:

Overall instructions. This chapter and Chapter 8 provide general instructions for using the Manual Maker. Soft copy of these two chapters is NOT provided on diskette, since you would not want to include them in your user manuals.

Divider and preface pages. These are found at the beginning of each chapter. They tell you what file contains the soft copy for the chapter and provide an overview of the chapter. These also give general ideas on how to modify the chapter. Soft copy of divider and preface pages is NOT provided on diskette because, again, you would not want to include them in your user manuals.

HOW TO USE THE NETWARE 286 MANUAL MAKER

Comments. These are scattered throughout the boilerplate text in both the hard and the soft copy. They are boxed to set them apart, like this:

> This is a comment.

The actual form that Comments take in the soft copy depends on what version (WordPerfect or ASCII) of the Manual Maker you are using, as you will see later. Naturally, you won't include Comments in your user manuals.

INTRODUCTION

Backing Up the Master Files

The very first thing you should do with the Manual Maker is to make a backup copy of the master diskettes and store them in a safe place; this is very important! Backing up doesn't take long, and it can save you a lot of grief. Take a few minutes and do it now.

Now that you've backed up the master diskettes, take a few minutes to skim through the rest of this chapter.

HOW TO USE THE NETWARE 286 MANUAL MAKER

What You Can Create with the Manual Maker

The basics of using the Manual Maker are simple: retrieve the soft copy boilerplate files and modify them to suit your needs. Once the files are modified, you have several options:

Create hard copy user manuals. Print your files, then duplicate, bind, and distribute the manuals as desired. This is a good choice if you have users who are new to computers and are not yet comfortable with working on-line. It is also a good choice if you don't have lots of users and the information in your manuals won't change often. But if you have a large number of users and the information in your manuals becomes outdated rapidly, you may want to consider one of the following choices.

Create an on-line manual. Put the files on your file server and flag them Read-Only so they can't be changed. Then decide how you want users to access the on-line manual and set it up accordingly. For example, if you want users to access the on-line manual from a menu, add an option to the menu (for example, "Manual") and tell users how to use that option.

Create on-line help. You can import the raw ASCII text from your modified files into an on-line Help facility so users can query the manual. This will be a lot of work, but it may be worth it if you have a lot of users to train.

INTRODUCTION

Using the Manual Maker: A Suggested Approach

I recommend that you work with the Manual Maker as follows:

First, make some preliminary decisions.

1. **Get an overview.** Scan the divider pages, preface pages, and actual text to get an overview of the material contained in the Manual Maker.

2. **Decide on different versions.** Decide if you want to create different versions of manuals for different users. Then, for each version of the manual that you want to create, complete these following steps.

3. **Choose a basic approach.** The Manual Maker is very flexible; the manuals you make with it can be as specific or as general as you want. The more specific you are, the more useful the manual is for your users. But this approach has some disadvantages, too. If you are very specific—for example, if you tell users their exact rights in certain directories—you will probably have to create different versions of the manual for different users. Also, your manuals may become outdated quickly if you change your network setup often.

4. **Copy and rename master files.** Make copies of the master files and rename the copies to avoid accidentally overwriting the masters. If you are creating more than one manual, use extensions to identify which manual the files will be used to create. For example, suppose you wanted to create a manual for beginning users and one for advanced users. You could name the files for the beginning users with a .BEG extension, and the files for the advanced users with a .ADV extension.

Now, start creating the manual(s).

HOW TO USE THE NETWARE 286 MANUAL MAKER

5. **Retrieve and modify soft copy.** Retrieve the soft copy file for the first chapter you want to include in your manual. Then modify the text to suit your needs, using the information contained in the divider pages, preface pages, and comments as guidelines.

   If you plan to include most of the text, just delete the material that you don't want; if you plan to delete most of the text, block copy the first chunk of material you want to include. Then switch to a second document (ALT-F3 for WordPerfect users), and retrieve the material into that document (Press ENTER for WordPerfect users). Save the second document and continue the process until you've copied all the material you want.

   Now go to the next chapter you want to include in your manual, and repeat steps 3 and 4. Continue until you have modified all the chapters you want to include in your user manual.

6. **Complete your formatting.** Turn to Chapter 8, "Instructions for Final Formatting," for instructions on how to finish your manual.

These are the basics. But before you begin, you should know a little more about the version of the Manual Maker files you are using (WordPerfect or ASCII).

INTRODUCTION

WordPerfect and ASCII Formats

The Manual Maker boilerplate files are provided in two formats, WordPerfect and ASCII. Which you use is a matter of personal preference. I recommend you use the WordPerfect format if at all possible, because then most of your formatting has been done for you; if you use the ASCII version, you'll have to do almost all of your own formatting.

For more information on formatting details, go to the appropriate section:

WordPerfect users—Continue with "Information for WordPerfect Users" on the next page.

ASCII users—Skip to "Information for ASCII Users," beginning on page 16.

HOW TO USE THE NETWARE 286 MANUAL MAKER

Information for WordPerfect Users

The more familiar you are with WordPerfect, the easier it will be for you to use the WordPerfect version of the Manual Maker. I have included instructions for everything you need to know.

The boilerplate hard copy contained in this book is very similar to the WordPerfect WordPerfect boilerplate files contained on the "WordPerfect" diskette that accompanies this book. However, there are some formatting details you need to be aware of.

Page size. The WordPerfect boilerplate files produce standard 10 point text on a standard 8.5 X 11 inch page with wide margins.

Comments. The boxed Comments shown on the screen will NOT print because they have been created with the WordPerfect Comments feature. The Comments you see in this book simulate those you will see on screen, however, you may note some minor discrepancies between the two.

The WordPerfect Comments feature lets you create text "windows" that don't take up vertical lines on the screen or print like regular text. Because of this, Comments provide a handy way to insert explanations, asides, questions, etc., into ordinary text—without having to delete these notes later. I used Comments to put notes in the boilerplate text for you, the supervisor, so that you wouldn't have to worry about deleting those notes from your user manuals.

INTRODUCTION

Comments can be turned on and off. In the boilerplate files that accompany this book, the Comments are turned on so you can see them as you modify the soft copy. But if you want to see how the pages look without the Comments—or how the pages print for your user manuals—just turn the Comments off (more on this later).

I also had to tweak the text to make the pagination in the soft copy files correspond with the pagination in the hard copy of the book. That is why most of the page breaks in the soft copy are hard page breaks. If you turn the Comments off, you may notice some blank and half-blank pages where the Comments were. The best way to handle this is to ignore any awkward page breaks until you have completed your manuals. Then turn the Comments off, page through the document, and delete any unnecessary hard page breaks (see Chapter 8, "Instructions for Final Formatting").

HOW TO USE THE NETWARE 286 MANUAL MAKER

Sequential Chapters and Page References. Chapter numbers, page numbers, and references are fine for conventional books, but I wasn't far into the Manual Maker before I realized they wouldn't work here. Why? Because I have no idea how you will modify the boilerplate text. My Chapter 6 may be your Chapter 3; your page numbers will almost certainly be different.

I tried to work around this problem in the following ways.

First, I kept the overall structure of the Manual Maker simple. For example, all the headings are at one level, because I don't know what you'll leave in or take out. In addition, when there was a choice between repeating material or cross-referencing, I usually repeated material. For this reason, you'll notice quite a bit of redundancy (the repetition of the rights table throughout Chapters 6 and 7 is a good example). If it bothers you, just delete the text you don't want.

Second, I did number the chapters and include some page references. However, chapter numbers are included in Comments so they won't print in your finished text. You can put chapter numbers in the manuals you create if you want to, of course. Just convert the desired Comments to regular text (position the cursor after the Comment, press CTRL-F5, choose Comment, choose Convert to Text). Then correct the numbering if necessary.

All page references have been created with the WordPerfect Cross-Reference feature. I used this feature to mark a reference and a target page for that reference. This allows accurate page references to be generated automatically. The page references you see in the hard copy and the initial on-line files are accurate for the generic Manual Maker before it is modified. After you create your own manuals, you must regenerate these page references. This should be the very last thing you do. See Chapter 8, "Instructions for Final Formatting," for the actual steps.

INTRODUCTION

Loosely Formatted Pages. Wherever possible, I divided the material in the Manual Maker up into small chunks of a page or less, titled the chunk, and started it on a new page. The Manual Maker material is not densely formatted; there are many pages with lots of white space. When you make your user manuals, you'll find that the pages condense quite a bit.

I formatted the material loosely for a couple of reasons. First, I wanted the Manual Maker to be easy to leaf through, both on-line and in the hard copy. I didn't want to make you search for headings in the middle of pages, or scroll through extraneous text on the screen to find something at the bottom of a page. Instead, I designed the Manual Maker so you can use Page Down (the Pg Dn key) and Go To (the CTRL-HOME keys) to "flip" to a page and see its title immediately.

Second, different computers and printers format pages differently. Because of this, a full page may be expanded slightly and become several pages, throwing pagination off.

Because the material is so loosely formatted, you may find yourself with blank and half-blank pages in the manuals you create. I suggest you handle this problem as follows. While you're creating the manual, just ignore any awkward page breaks. Then, after you finish modifying the manual, use the Search (F2) key to find the hard page breaks, and delete those you don't want (see Chapter 8, "Instructions for Final Formatting").

You can format your manuals as densely as you want; but I suggest that you keep one topic to a page where feasible. Manuals that chunk material this way and begin each topic on a new page are easier to use.

HOW TO USE THE NETWARE 286 MANUAL MAKER

Information for ASCII Users

The ASCII files are included for your use if you prefer not to use WordPerfect. They can be imported into the text editor or word processor of your choice. If you choose to use the ASCII files, you'll have to do almost all of your own formatting, since the ASCII text doesn't contain any formatting codes.

In addition to doing your own formatting, you'll also need to be aware of the following details.

Notes to Supervisors. The Manual Maker boilerplate text is sprinkled liberally with notes to supervisors. In the hard copy, these notes can be identified by the boxes that surround them. In the ASCII text, these notes are labeled with COMMENT BEGIN at the beginning of the comment, and COMMENT END immediately following the comment. These codes are included so that you can easily identify the notes and delete them after you have completed your manuals (see Chapter 8, "Instructions for Final Formatting"). You can delete the notes manually, of course; but if macros are available in your text editor or word processor, it's much easier to use them. Your macro should look something like this:

    Find COMMENT BEGIN
    Move to beginning of the word "COMMENT"
    Turn Block on
    Find COMMENT END
    Delete Block

INTRODUCTION

Sequential Chapters and Page References. Normally, books have chapter numbers, page numbers, and references that depend on a sequential structure. This is fine for conventional books, but I wasn't far into the Manual Maker before I realized it wouldn't work here. Why? Because I have no idea how you will modify the boilerplate text. My Chapter 6 may be your Chapter 3; your page numbers will almost certainly be different.

I tried to work around this problem in the following ways.

First, I tried to keep the overall structure of the Manual Maker simple. For example, all the headings are at the same level, because I don't know what you'll leave in or take out. In addition, when there was a choice between repeating material or cross-referencing, I usually repeated material. For this reason, you'll notice quite a bit of redundancy (the repetition of the Rights Table throughout Chapters 6 and 7 is a good example). If the redundancy bothers you, just delete the text you don't want.

Second, I did number the chapters and include some page references. However, all of these references are included in the notes to supervisors. So when you delete the notes to supervisors, the references will also be deleted. You can leave these references in, of course; just make sure you haven't deleted the text that the reference cites, and be sure to change numerical references if necessary.

HOW TO USE THE NETWARE 286 MANUAL MAKER

Loosely Formatted Pages. Wherever possible, I divided the material in the Manual Maker up into small chunks of a page or less, and start each chunk on a new page. The Manual Maker material isn't densely formatted; you'll notice many pages with lots of white space. When you make your user manuals, you'll find that the pages condense quite a bit.

I formatted the material loosely for a couple of reasons. First, I wanted the Manual Maker to be easy to leaf through, both on-line and in the hard copy. I didn't want to make you search for headings in the middle of pages, or scroll through extraneous text on the screen to find something at the bottom of a page. Instead, I designed the Manual Maker so you can "flip" to a page on-line and see its title immediately.

Second, different computers and printers format pages differently. Because of this, a full page may be expanded slightly and become several pages, throwing pagination off.

Because the material is so loosely formatted, you may find yourself with blank and half-blank pages in the manuals you create. I suggest you handle this problem as follows. While you're creating the manual, just ignore any awkward page breaks. Then, when you are finished modifying the manual, use your word processor's Search key to find the hard page breaks, and delete those you don't want. (See Chapter 8, "Instructions for Final Formatting.")

You can format your manuals as densely as you want; but I suggest that you keep one topic to a page where feasible. (Manuals that chunk material this way and begin each topic on a new page are easier to use.)

CHAPTER OVERVIEW

Introduction to Networking and Netware

The text for this boilerplate chapter is found in
INTRO.WP (WordPerfect version)
INTRO.ASC (ASCII version)

22	**What is a Network?**
22	**Template: An Overview of Our Network** Gives users a general overview.
23	**Essential Network Components** Explains file servers, workstations, adapters, drivers, and cabling.
26	**Peripherals**
27	**Template: A Description of Our Network** Used to give users a more detailed description of your network—details on how many file servers and workstations, the types of hardware, etc.

CHAPTER 1

Introduction to Networking and Netware

> This chapter introduces the basics of networking and NetWare via simple, generic overviews. The material given here is intended mainly for new NetWare users who need an overall, high-level orientation.
>
> I suggest that you include this chapter in all your user materials, because it provides the background context for further training. However, feel free to customize the information based on how your network is set up and administered, what you want to teach your users, and what they already know. Ideas for doing this are included throughout the text.

THE NETWARE 286 MANUAL MAKER

What is a Network?

> Explains what networks are and why they're useful.

A network is a group of computers connected together so that the people using them can communicate and share resources. Networks can greatly increase an organization's efficiency and cost-effectivenss.

> Template: An Overview of Our Network
>
> You can use the following template to give users a very general overview of how you're using networks. Modify the template to suit your needs.

At <substitute your organization name here>, we use networks to <list purposes of your network—link personal computers, access on-line services, etc.>.

Our network spans <physical area the network covers—building, nationwide, international, etc.> There are <number> of <type> computers connected to our network.

About <number> people from <number or names of> divisions work on the network. On our networks, we're doing <describe the kind of work being done on your networks>.

We decided to use networks because <list your reasons for implementing networks>. We've been using networks since <general time period when you first installed networks at your organization>. We plan to <describe future plans for networking in your organization—keep it pretty general at this point>.

INTRODUCTION TO NETWORKING AND NETWARE

Essential Network Components

> Explains the essential components of a NetWare network and what they do.

Networks vary greatly in their actual physical setup and complexity. But regardless of their size or complexity, all NetWare networks have at least the following essential components:

File servers—personal computers which store network applications and network data. (Application—software which manages specialized tasks, like word processing or accounting.)

> You may wish to list some applications which your users are familiar with as examples here.

File servers also run the NetWare operating system, which manages the network's operation. (Operating system—software which manages a computer's inner workings so you can use the computer's services.)

> Ideas for presenting and customizing this material: (A template which you can use to customize users' written manuals is found on page 27.)
>
> - Show users a file server.
> - Tell users how many file servers are on your network.
> - Tell users what applications are being used on your network.
> - Include or delete the definition of "application" and "operating system" depending on your users' level of experience and what you want to teach them.

NETWORK USER'S GUIDE   23

THE NETWARE 286 MANUAL MAKER

Workstations—personal computers where you and other network users do your work. Workstations enable you to access the applications and data which are on the file server. Workstations then run the applications and process the data using their own operating systems.

Workstations also run a piece of software called the NetWare shell, which decides if requests made at the workstation should be handled by the workstation's operating system or by NetWare, and routes the requests accordingly.

Ideas for presenting and customizing this material:

(A template which you can use to customize the users' written manuals is found on page 27.)

- Show users some of the workstations on your network, or explain where they are (on individual desks, grouped according to functions, etc.) Tell them where the workstation(s) they'll be using are located.

- Tell users how many workstations are on the network.

- Tell users what network applications they'll be using and how they will access those applications (or tell them that you'll be covering this information and when you'll be covering it).

- Tell users what operating system the workstation runs (DOS in most cases), and that they can still use most of the commands they would use if they were using that machine as a standalone personal computer.

INTRODUCTION TO NETWORKING AND NETWARE

Network adapters—printed circuit boards which are inserted into every file server and workstation on the network.

LAN drivers—software which, along with network adapters, prepares information to travel between file servers and workstations.

Cabling and other hardware—physically connects the workstations and file servers into a network.

Ideas for presenting and customizing this material:

(A template which you can use to customize the users' written manuals is found on page 27.)

- Show a network adapter; explain how it's inserted into a PC.

- Show how network adapters are connected to cabling to attach a station to the network.

- Show users the hardware your network uses (cabling, BNC connectors, passive/active hubs, MAUs, etc.).

NETWORK USER'S GUIDE   25

THE NETWARE 286 MANUAL MAKER

Network Peripherals

> Explains peripherals and introduces common network peripherals.

Peripherals are physical resources which are part of the network. Peripherals are optional; the network can run without them. But some peripherals are essential for most network users. (Printers are a good example.) Peripherals may be located throughout the network.

Common peripherals include:

- **Printers**

- **Disk subsystems**—external hard disks attached to the file server to expand its disk space.

- **Uninterruptible Power Supplies**—provide temporary power to the file server if the regular power supply goes off unexpectedly, and protect the server against power fluctuations.

- **Tape backup units**—back up network files.

Ideas for presenting and customizing this material:

(A template which you can use to customize the users' written manuals is found on page 27.)

- Tell users what peripherals your network has, what services the peripherals provide, and which peripherals they'll use.

- Tell them where the printers are (especially the printers they'll be using).

---

26   NETWARE USER'S GUIDE

INTRODUCTION TO NETWORKING AND NETWARE

> Template: A Description of Our Network
>
> You can use the following template to give users a description of your network. Modify the template to suit your needs.

A Description of Our Network

Here's a quick description of our network.

File Servers: <number and hardware type>

Connection hardware:

Network adapters: <type—Ethernet, Arcnet, etc.>

Cabling scheme: <type—Token ring, Star, etc.>

Peripherals: <list peripherals and purpose of each; tell users which they will use; if necessary, also list location, especially for peripherals like printers>

Workstations: <number and type on network>

Workstation you will use: <type, location>

Workstation operating system:

Applications on the network: <general (word processing, spreadsheets, etc.) or specific (WordPerfect, 1-2-3, etc.)>

Applications you will use: <specific applications the user will use>

THE NETWARE 286 MANUAL MAKER

Conclusion

> Summarize what you covered and introduce what will be covered next. A sample conclusion for this generic chapter is included next. Change it based on how you changed the chapter.

Now you know what a network is and what our network is like. The next step is to learn how to work on the network, starting with logging in.

CHAPTER OVERVIEW

Logging In and Out

The text for this boilerplate chapter is found in
LOGIN.WP (WordPerfect version)
LOGIN.ASC (ASCII version)

31		**Why You Have to Log In**
32		**How to Log In**
		Gives three approaches to logging in.
38		**What You See After You Log In**
39		**Batch Files and Login Scripts**
		Explains the role these play in determining what users see when they log in.
40		**A Basic Display**
		Explains the display created by the default login script.
42		**Custom Menus**
53		**Logging In to More than One Server at a Time**
54		**How to Change Your Password**
56		**Logging Out**
57		**Conclusion**

29

CHAPTER 2

Getting On and Off the Network: Logging In and Out

This chapter explains how to log in and out and how to change a password. (Account and other restrictions are explained in the next chapter.)

Why You Have to Log In

Before you can use the network, you must log in. Requiring you to log in is the network's way of identifying you so it can enforce network security and track your network activity. Logging in is the first level of NetWare security, since it controls who may access the network. Once you've logged in, you can work on the network within the limits of your network security and other restrictions.

The instructions in this chapter assume that your users

- Know where the CTRL, ALT, and DEL keys are located on their keyboards

- Know what it means to boot a computer

- Are at least somewhat familiar with working on a computer (they know they must press ENTER to execute a command, etc.)

If you have novice users who are brand new to personal computers, you may need to add some material to this chapter.

THE NETWARE 286 MANUAL MAKER

How to Log In

Here are the steps involved in logging in.

> Start with one of the basic approaches given next, then customize based on how your network is set up and how much information you want to give your users.

> Approach #1:
>
> I recommend this approach for new users who just want to get on the network and don't need to know much about what's going on. This explanation is tailored for use with the following AUTOEXEC.BAT file.
>
> Echo off
> IPX > NUL
> NET3 > NUL
> F:
> prompt pg
> Login username

1. Turn on your machine if necessary.

2. Press CTRL-ALT-DEL to boot your machine.

   When you do this, the machine loads the workstation's operating system and runs the AUTOEXEC.BAT file (if one exists), just as it would if it weren't on the network.

   After that, some commands will be executed automatically to establish a connection with the network and log you in. You will see some network information, and then you'll be prompted for your password.

GETTING ON AND OFF THE NETWORK: LOGGING IN AND OUT

3. Enter your password when prompted.

   If you enter your password incorrectly, the network won't log you in. If this happens, you will have to type

   LOGIN *username*

   and then enter your password when prompted.

Approach #2:

I recommend this approach for curious users who need to learn how to log in, but also want to know what's going on. This explanation is tailored for use with the following AUTOEXEC.BAT file.

Echo off
IPX
NET3
f:
Prompt pg
Login username

---

1. Turn on your machine.

2. Press CTRL-ALT-DEL to boot your machine.

   When you do this, the machine loads the workstation's operating system and runs the AUTOEXEC.BAT file (if one exists).

   What you'll see next is explained in the following table.

NETWORK USER'S GUIDE

THE NETWARE 286 MANUAL MAKER

What You See	What It Means
A>IPX	IPX, the software that allows the network adapter to talk to the shell, is being loaded.
Version, revision, and copyright information for IPX	
A>NETX	NET2, NET3, or NET4 is loaded next, depending on the version of DOS that you're using. This is the portion of the shell that communicates with DOS.
Version, revision, and copyright information for NETX	
Attached to server *Servername* Date Time	The server you've attached to and when you attached to it.
A>F:	A pointer is being set up to the area of the file server's hard disk where the commands that let you log in are located.
F:\LOGIN>login *username* Enter your password:	You are being logged in as user *username* and now need to enter your password.

GETTING ON AND OFF THE NETWORK: LOGGING IN AND OUT

3. Enter your password to finish logging in.

   If you enter your password incorrectly, the network won't log you in. If this happens, you will have to type

   > LOGIN *username*

and then enter your password as prompted.

THE NETWARE 286 MANUAL MAKER

> Approach #3: Logging In Manually
>
> I don't recommend this approach. It doesn't make much sense to have users log in manually when you can use an AUTOEXEC.BAT file. But if you choose not to create an AUTOEXEC.BAT file for some reason, use this explanation.

1. Turn on your machine.

2. Press CTRL-ALT-DEL to boot your machine.

   When you do this, the machine does everything it would do even if you weren't using it on the network. It performs a self-check, runs the CONFIG.SYS file, and loads COMMAND.COM.

3. Type

   IPX

   This loads IPX, the software that allows the network adapter to talk to the shell.

4. Type

   ANET2
   ANET3
   ANET4

> Choose the appropriate command for the version of DOS the user is using: ANET2 for DOS 2.X, ANET3 for DOS 3.X, ANET4 for DOS 4.X. Then delete the other two commands.

GETTING ON AND OFF THE NETWORK: LOGGING IN AND OUT

This step loads the NetWare shell, that communicates between DOS and NetWare.

5. Type

   F:

   This points you to the area of the file server's hard disk that contains the commands you need to log in.

6. Type

LOGIN *username*

7. Enter your password.

NETWORK USER'S GUIDE

THE NETWARE 286 MANUAL MAKER

What You See After You Log In

> You can take several approaches here.
>
> 1. Simply tell users what they'll see when they log in.
>
> 2. Explain why they see what they see when they log in.
>
> 3. Do something in between.
>
>   In addition, it's very likely that you will need to customize this section according to what you have done with batch files, login scripts, and menus. This section consists of building blocks along with ideas for when each building block might be used. Pick, choose, and modify according to your needs.

GETTING ON AND OFF THE NETWORK: LOGGING IN AND OUT

Batch Files and Login Scripts

> This section explains how batch files and login scripts determine what users see when they log in. Include it if you have curious users who are sophisticated enough to understand the information and would like to learn about it—especially users who might like to tinker with their own login scripts and batch files. (Provided, of course, that you are comfortable with them doing so.)

Several files determine what you see after you log in.

- **Login scripts** contain commands that help prepare your workstation to work with NetWare. There are several types of login scripts: a system login script, which applies to everyone, and your personal login script, which applies just to you.

> Technically speaking, there is also a third type of login script. A default login script is actually part of the LOGIN.EXE program. The default login script is executed if a user doesn't have a personal login script. It is the same login script you see when you log in as Supervisor for the first time. Users probably don't need to know about this login script.

When you log in, the system login script is executed first. Then your personal login script is executed.

- **Batch files** provide a convenient way of executing commands in "bunches." When the batch file's name is typed, the commands it contains are executed. Batch files provide a convenient shortcut; if a certain series of commands is executed routinely, it can be put in a batch file to automate the process.

> If you want to, you can show users their login scripts and batch files now. This may be better saved until after they have taken a look around the network, however.

NETWORK USER'S GUIDE

THE NETWARE 286 MANUAL MAKER

A Basic Display

> This section explains the basic display that is set up by the default login script as part of the LOGIN.EXE program. This default login script is executed if a user doesn't have a personal login script. If there is a system login script, but no personal login script, this default login script will fill in any "holes" that the system login script leaves out.
>
> It's unlikely that a user would see a display exactly like that explained in this section, but you can use the information given here as a starting point to explain what the user does see. You can also customize this section as explained in the next comment.

> To customize this section so it shows the display the user really sees,
>
> 1. Log in as the user.
>
> 2. Create a screen dump in the file DISPLAY by typing
>
>   CAPTURE CR=DISPLAY
>
>   (Note: the user must have the Create right in the current directory for this to work)
>
> 3. Press the SHIFT and PRT SC keys simultaneously.
>
> 4. Retrieve the file DISPLAY into this section (SHIFT F10, filename for WordPerfect users).
>
> 5. Clean up the display by deleting the extraneous parts of the screen dump. HINT: Setting margins to .1, .1 eliminates unwanted doublespacing.

GETTING ON AND OFF THE NETWORK: LOGGING IN AND OUT

> If you customize this section to show the actual screen display that the user sees, you may also want to customize the following generic explanation. (Note that this explanation assumes that users know what directory structures are; if they don't, you may want to skip over it and tell them that you'll explain the display later.)

Here's what you see when you log in, and what it means.

Display	Meaning
Good evening, USERNAME.	A greeting to you.
Drive A: maps to a local disk. Drive B: maps to a local disk. Drive C: maps to a local disk. Drive D: maps to a local disk. Drive E: maps to a local disk. Drive F: = LATE\SYS: \	These are drive mappings. Drive mappings point to different storage areas on the file server's hard disk.
SEARCH1: = Z:. [LATE\SYS: \PUBLIC] SEARCH2: = Y:. [LATE\SYS: \]	These are search drive mappings. They tell the system where to look if it can't find a file you request in your current directory.

NETWORK USER'S GUIDE

THE NETWARE 286 MANUAL MAKER

Custom Menus

If you have created a custom menu that is displayed when the user logs in, explain the menu here.

The next few sections contain examples of some simple custom menus you might use. They also explain how to create these menus with the NetWare MENU utility, then call the menus from the user's login script.

Here's a quick refresher on how to create a menu with NetWare's MENU utility, then call the menu from a login script so it will appear when the user logs in.

1. Make a text file to create the menu. Observe these rules:

   Menu title—first in the file, preceded by a % sign, flush left

   Menu options—Type flush left

   What the option does—type immediately following option, indented

2. Save the file in ASCII format with a .MNU extension.

3. Include this command at the end of the user's login script:

   #MENU *filename*

NETWORK USER'S GUIDE

GETTING ON AND OFF THE NETWORK: LOGGING IN AND OUT

Notes on menus for supervisors:

If users can't access the files that create their menus, program execution will fail when the menu is called. For a user to access a file,

1. The .MNU file that creates the menu must be in the user's current directory or a directory mapped to a search drive.

2. The user must have Read, Open, and Search rights for the .MNU file.

If you will be using lots of menus, you may want to create a specific directory for .MNU files. Then, in the system login script, map a search drive to that directory, and use SYSCON to give the group EVERYONE Read, Open, and Search rights in the directory.

NETWORK USER'S GUIDE   43

THE NETWARE 286 MANUAL MAKER

Sample Menu #1: Applications

This section explains how to create a simple menu that users can use to access their applications. This is a good menu for users that you want to shield from **NetWare as** much **as possible.**

The explanation of how to create the menu is given on this page. This explanation is for you, as supervisor, and should not be included in the user's manual. The explanation to include in the user's manual after this explanation.

To create a custom menu to access applications, complete these steps.

1. First, make an ASCII text file to create the menu. Here is the basic format to use:

   %MenuTitle
      Application1
      Echo off
      CLS
      command to access application1
   Application2
      Echo off
      CLS
      command to access application2
   Logout
      !logout

GETTING ON AND OFF THE NETWORK: LOGGING IN AND OUT

For example:

%Applications I Use
WordPerfect
    Echo off
    CLS
    WP
Lotus 1-2-3
    Echo off
    CLS
    123
Logout
    !logout

2. Save this file as an ASCII file with a .MNU extension—for example, APPS.MNU.

3. Call the menu from the user's login script by using this command at the end of the login script:

#MENU *path:filename*

For example, to call the menu created by APPS.MNU, at the end of the user's login script, include this command:

#MENU *path:APPS*

THE NETWARE 286 MANUAL MAKER

> Explanation to include in user's manual for Sample Menu #1:
>
> This is the explanation you would include in the user manual—customized to your particular menu, of course.

Use the following menu to access your applications:

<Type menu here, just as it appears to the user>

<After the menu, explain each menu item—what it is, why and how it would be used, etc.>

When you are finished working in your application, exit as usual. You are returned to this menu.

When you are finished working, highlight the "Logout" option and press ENTER to exit the system.

GETTING ON AND OFF THE NETWORK: LOGGING IN AND OUT

Sample Menu #2: Applications ... and then some

In the previous example, all of the user's files are dumped into the same directory—wherever the user was when the applications were accessed.

This example shows how to create a menu that automatically moves the user to a given directory when an application is accessed. That way, you can ensure that all files of a certain type are placed in the same directory.

This example is probably a little simple-minded in actual practice, but it illustrates the basic principle. Modify it to suit your needs.

Here is the explanation for you, as supervisor. Do not include this explanation in the user's manual—unless you want the user to be able to create his or her own menus.

To create a custom menu used to access applications, and that moves the user to a given directory upon accessing a certain application, complete these steps.

1. First, make an ASCII text file to create the menu. Here's the basic format to use:

   %MenuTitle
   Application1
      Echo Off
      CLS
      CD *desired directory*
      command to access application1
   Application2
      Echo Off
      CLS

NETWORK USER'S GUIDE

THE NETWARE 286 MANUAL MAKER

    CD *desired directory*
    command to access application2
Logout
    !logout

For example:

%Diana's Menu
    WordPerfect
    Echo Off
    CLS
    CD \Home\Diana\WPfiles
    WP
Lotus 1-2-3
    Echo Off
    CLS
    CD \Home\Diana\123files
    123
Logout
    !logout

2. Save this file as an ASCII file with a .MNU extension—for example, DIANA.MNU.

3. Call the menu from the user's login script by using this command at the end of the login script:

    #MENU *path:filename*

For example, to call the menu created by DIANA.MNU, at the end of the user's login script, include this command:

    #MENU SYS:MENUS:DIANA

GETTING ON AND OFF THE NETWORK: LOGGING IN AND OUT

> Explanation to include in user's manual for **Sample Menu #2**:
>
> This is the explanation you would include in the user manual—customized to your particular menu, of course. It is the same as the explanation for the previous menu, because to the user, the two menus look about the same.

Use the following menu to access your applications:

<Type menu here, just as it appears to the user>

<After the menu, explain each menu item—what it is, why and how it would be used, etc.>

When you are finished working in your application, exit as usual. You are returned to this menu.

When you are finished working, highlight the "Logout" option and press ENTER to exit the system.

NETWORK USER'S GUIDE

THE NETWARE 286 MANUAL MAKER

Sample Menu #3: The NetWare Menu Utilities

This example explains how to create a simple menu which users can use to access the most commonly-used NetWare menu utilities. If you want to limit your users' access to the NetWare interface, and feel that menu utilities are the best bet, you might use a menu similar to the one in this section. (In actual practice, you would probably also include options to access applications—making your real menu a combination of this menu and a menu in one of the previous examples.)

You can choose which utilities you want to include in the menu, of course. I've included SYSCON, SESSION, FILER, and PCONSOLE in the example, but SYSCON and FILER are sufficient for most users.

Here is the explanation for you, as supervisor. Do not include this explanation in the user's manual—unless you want the user to be able to create his or her own menus.

To create a custom menu used to access the NetWare menu utilities, complete the steps on the next page.

GETTING ON AND OFF THE NETWORK: LOGGING IN AND OUT

1. First, make an ASCII text file to create the menu.

```
%NetWare Utilities
SYSCON
   Echo off
   CLS
   SYSCON
FILER
   Echo off
   CLS
   FILER
SESSION
   Echo off
   CLS
   SESSION
PCONSOLE
   Echo off
   CLS
   PCONSOLE
Logout
   !logout
```

2. Save this file with a .MNU extension—for example, NETUTILS.MNU.

3. Call the menu from the user's login script by using this command at the end of the login script:

   #MENU *path:NETUTILS*

NETWORK USER'S GUIDE   51

THE NETWARE 286 MANUAL MAKER

> Explanation to include in user's manual for Sample Menu 3:
>
> Here are some ideas of what you might want to include in the user's manual if you had created a menu just like the one in the previous example.

Use this menu to access the NetWare menu utilities.

To access a utility, use the arrow keys to highlight it. Then press ENTER.

When you are finished working in the utility, exit by pressing ESCAPE and answering "Yes" when prompted to exit the utility. You are then returned to this menu.

When you are finished working, highlight the "Logout" option and press ENTER to exit the system.

> Here you may include documentation for the utilities themselves if you wish. You can copy what you want from the reference chapter on the NetWare menu utilities, and place it here. If you do this, you may want to eliminate the menu utilities and command line utilities reference sections from the user's manual.

GETTING ON AND OFF THE NETWORK: LOGGING IN AND OUT

Logging In to More than One Server at a Time

> Include this section only if
>
> - There is more than one file server on the **network**.
>
> - The user has an account on more than one of the servers

Sometimes you may need to work on more than one server at a time. If this is the case, you'll need to log in to all the servers you need to work on. Here is how to do so.

1. Log in to your regular server as usual.

2. If you know the name of the server you want to log in to, and your username on that server, type

   ATTACH *servername/username*

   For example, if you wanted to attach to server GADFLY as user Steve, type

   ATTACH GADFLY/STEVE

   If you don't know the name of the server, use the SLIST command to list the servers on the network. Type

   SLIST

   You'll see a list of servers on the network. Pick the server you want to log in to, then type

   ATTACH *servername/username*

3. You'll probably be prompted for a password after you enter your username. Enter the password at the prompt.

NETWORK USER'S GUIDE

THE NETWARE 286 MANUAL MAKER

How to Change Your Password

There are several ways to change your password.

Include the ways that are relevant.

1. Include either the menu or command line method depending whether your users use menu or command line NetWare commands.

2. If you don't force password changes, delete the next paragraph.

- **Forced change.** On our network, you must change your password periodically. The network tells you when you need to change your password. You'll get a message telling you that your password has expired. When you are prompted to enter a new password, type your new password at the "Enter new password" prompt; then re-type it when prompted. You must observe any password restrictions that apply, such as minimum length or uniqueness.

You may or may not want to tell your users about grace logins, if they apply. The disadvantage in doing so is that if users know about grace logins, they tend to put off changing their passwords and then get locked out.

If you want to tell users about grace logins, you can use the following sample text.

When you are prompted to change your password, you have a certain number of "grace" logins during which you can still use the old password to log in. Once you run out of grace logins, you will be locked out from the server. For this reason, it is best to make a habit of changing your password right away.

54   NETWORK USER'S GUIDE

GETTING ON AND OFF THE NETWORK: LOGGING IN AND OUT

- **Voluntary change.** Sometimes you will want to change your password of your own accord.

> Include this method if users have access to the command line.

To change your password voluntarily,

1. Type

   SETPASS

2. Enter your new password when prompted.

3. Re-enter your new password when prompted.

> Include this method if users only have access to the menu utilities.

1. Access SYSCON.

2. Choose "User Information."

3. Choose your name.

4. Choose "Change Password."

5. Enter your new password.

6. Re-enter your new password.

NETWORK USER'S GUIDE   55

THE NETWARE 286 MANUAL MAKER

Logging Out

When you are finished working on the network, you should always log out—just like you lock the door when you leave the house so intruders cannot get in. In fact, you should log out from the network if you're going to leave your workstation for any length of time. This prevents potentially malicious users from using network resources or accessing your personal data.

> Include this method if users log out from the command line.

To log out, type

> LOGOUT

You see a message telling you when you logged out and what server(s) you logged out from.

> Include this method if users log out from a custom menu and you haven't already covered how to log out when you explained how to use the menu.

To log out,

1. Use the arrow keys to highlight the "Logout" option.

2. Press ENTER.

> You see a message telling you when you logged out and what server(s) you logged out from.

GETTING ON AND OFF THE NETWORK: LOGGING IN AND OUT

Conclusion

> The following sample conclusion and transition is based on the generic information in this chapter. If you include it, modify it according to how you modified the chapter and what you will cover next.

In this chapter, you learned

- How to log in to the network

- What you see when you log in to the network

- How to use batch files and login scripts

- How to use menus

- How to attach to another file server

- How to change your password

- How to log out

Now that you have logged in, we'll start looking around the network.

CHAPTER OVERVIEW

Network Restrictions

The text for this boilerplate chapter is found in
RESTRICT.WP (WordPerfect version)
RESTRICT.ASC (ASCII version)

62 **Account Restrictions**

  Explains restrictions on the user's account (login restrictions, time restrictions, etc.). Choose one of the two approaches:
  - 63 Tell the user about the restrictions.
  - 65 Show and explain the restrictions.

68 **Disk Space Restrictions**

  Explains disk restrictions. Choose one of the three approaches:
  - 68 Tell the user about the restrictions.
  - 69 Show and explain the restrictions.
  - 70 Force the user to check space usage periodically.

CHAPTER 3

Network Restrictions

> This chapter explains some of the restrictions that may apply to your users. (It does NOT explain security; security is explained in the next chapters.) The chapter is divided into two sections:
>
> 1. Account restrictions (limit when and how users can log in)
>
> 2. Disk restrictions (limit how much space users can consume on the file server)
>
> Choose the material you want to include based on the restrictions you have established for your network, and what you want your users to know about those restrictions.

Because a network is a shared environment, there are many restrictions that control how you work on it. This chapter explains the restrictions that apply to you on our network.

THE NETWARE 286 MANUAL MAKER

> Section 1: Account Restrictions

Login Restrictions

> If you have set up account restrictions, it is important to explain them to your users. This will save them the frustration of trying to log in during unauthorized time periods, etc. It may also save you the frustration of having to solve problems caused because users don't understand their restrictions.

On our network, there are some restrictions that affect when and how you can log in. You need to know about these restrictions so they won't get in your way.

> You can take a couple of approaches to explaining the restrictions:
>
> You can just tell your users what they are, or
>
> You can show your users how to see the restrictions, then explain what they mean.
>
> Sample sections for each approach are included next.

NETWORK RESTRICTIONS

> Approach #1 (Login Restrictions):
> Tell users what their login restrictions are.
>
> This section lists login restrictions that might apply to users. Delete the restrictions that don't apply. Then insert the appropriate information as instructed by the notes within the angle brackets.

Here are the login restrictions that apply to you and what they mean.

> While you are filling in the blanks in the next section, you may want to look at the information in SYSCON. To do so,
>
> 1. Access SYSCON.
>
> 2. Account restrictions—default or individual user
>
> 2a. If you have established default account restrictions that apply to everyone on your server, choose "Supervisor Options." Then choose "Default Account Balance/ Restrictions."
>
> 2b. If you have established account restrictions on a user-by-user basis, choose "User Information." Then choose the user name, and "Account Restrictions."
>
> (If you have done this, you must modify the next section in each user's manual separately so that the manuals are accurate.)

    Expiration date. After <insert the date here>, you won't be able to log in to the network any more.

    Number of workstations. You can only be logged in to the file server from <insert the number of stations here> workstations at a time.

NETWORK USER'S GUIDE

THE NETWARE 286 MANUAL MAKER

Password requirements : Passwords <are, aren't> required on our network.

Changing your password. You <can, cannot> change your own password.

Minimum password length. Your password must be at least <number> characters long.

Periodic password changes. You must change your password every <number> days. You will be prompted when it's time to change your password.

Grace logins. When it comes time to change your password, it's best to do so right away. You will still be allowed <number> grace logins, when you can still log in with the old password. If you don't change your password before your grace logins are used up, you will be unable to log in to the network. Then you'll have to come to <name of their supervisor, account manager, workgroup manager, help desk, etc.> for help.

Unique passwords. You <can, cannot> use a password you've used before.

Station restrictions. You can only log in from certain workstations. <Tell them which ones.>

Time restrictions. You can only log in to the network and use it during the following time periods:
<List the time periods here. Modify the following sample text.>

Day	Time
Sun	
Mon	
Tues	
Weds	
Thurs	
Fri	
Sat	

NETWORK RESTRICTIONS

> Approach #2 (Login Restrictions):
> Tell users how to see their login restrictions and explain what the restrictions mean as they go along.
>
> NOTE: This approach will work only if you have set up account restrictions for the user specifically, using the "User Information" option in SYSCON. If you have used the "Supervisor Options" option to set up restrictions for all users, users will not be able to see the restrictions, because users cannot access the information under the "Supervisor Options" menu option.

To see your login restrictions, choose the method that applies or modify as desired.

- At the DOS prompt, type SYSCON and press ENTER.
  or
- Choose SYSCON from the menu.

1. Choose "User Information."

2. Choose your name.

3. Choose "Account Restrictions."

Here are the restrictions that apply to you and what they mean.

Disable account. Your account can be disabled so that you cannot log in, but this is rare.

Expiration date. If this says "Yes," you won't be able to log in after the date specified under "Date Account Expires."

NETWORK USER'S GUIDE

THE NETWARE 286 MANUAL MAKER

Limit Concurrent Connections. If this says "Yes," you can only be logged in to the number of workstations specified under "Maximum Connections."

Allow User to Change Password. If this says "Yes," you can change your password.

Require Password. If this says "Yes," you must enter a password to log in. The restrictions that apply to your password are next:

Minimum Password Length. The number of characters your password must have.

Force Periodic Password Changes. If you select "Yes," you must change your password periodically. The amount of time between password changes is shown in the next field, "Days Between Forced Changes." The date your password expires, and if you will have to specify a new one, is shown in the field "Date Password Expires."

Limit Grace Logins. If this says "Yes," you have a certain number of "grace" logins when you can still use the old password before changing it. The number of grace logins is shown next to "Grace Logins Allowed," and the number you have left is shown next to "Remaining Grace Logins."

Require Unique Passwords. If this says "Yes," you cannot use a password you've used before when you specify a new password.

5. Now press ESCAPE.

NETWORK RESTRICTIONS

6. Choose "Station Restrictions."

This shows you the addresses of the workstations you're allowed to log in from.

> Unfortunately, station addresses don't mean much to most users. If you have restricted the workstations they can log in from, it is probably best to just tell them where they are allowed to log in from.

7. Press ESCAPE.

8. Choose "Time Restrictions."

This shows you the times you are allowed to log in. The time periods that have asterisks are the time periods when you can log in or be logged in; the time periods without asterisks are the time periods when you cannot log in or be logged in on the network.

9. Press ALT-F10 and answer "Yes" to exit SYSCON.

THE NETWARE 286 MANUAL MAKER

Section 2: Disk Restrictions

Disk Restrictions

> Include this section if
>
> - You have limited the disk space available to the user.
>
> - You wish to tell your users about this restriction.
>
> This section offers the same approaches as before:
>
> 1. Tell the user what the restrictions are.
>
> 2. Tell the user how to see the restrictions and what they mean.
>
> A third alternative—executing the CHKVOL command from the system login script so that users automatically monitor their restrictions periodically—is also explained.

Approach #1: (Disk Restrictions)

Tell users what their restrictions are.

On our network, there are some restrictions on how much total disk space you can use.

Here are the restrictions that apply to you:

On file server <server name>, you can use <number> Kilobytes of space.

If you reach this limit, you won't be able to save files. You will have to go back and delete some of your old files to free up space before you can save files again.

NETWORK RESTRICTIONS

> Approach #2: (Disk Restrictions)
>
> Show users how to see their restrictions and explain what they mean as you go along.

On our network, there are some restrictions on how much total disk space you can use.

To see your space restrictions,

1. At the DOS prompt, type

    SYSCON

2. Choose "User Information."

3. Choose your name.

4. Choose "Account Restrictions."

5. You'll then see how much space is available to you (near the bottom of the screen).

If you use up all of your space, you won't be able to save files. You will have to go back and delete some of your old files to free up space before you can save files again.

NETWORK USER'S GUIDE   **69**

THE NETWARE 286 MANUAL MAKER

Approach #3: (Disk Restrictions)

Forcing Users to Check Periodically

The main reason to tell users about their disk restrictions is so that they won't run out of space—or if they do, they'll have some idea of what's going on. Of course, it's better to be proactive than reactive. There are a couple of ways to do this.

You can use SYSCON to monitor users' network usage yourself. Then, when they get close to their space limits, send them a warning message telling them that they're running out of space, and need to delete their old files.

You can also include CHKVOL in users' login scripts to force them to check their restrictions periodically themselves. This section explains how to do so, and gives you a template to use in your user manuals if you take this approach.

Of course, if you give users this responsibility, you should make sure they're up to it. It won't help them much to know that they're approaching their space limit if they don't have the Delete right in at least some of the directories they work in, because they won't be able to clean up old files anyway. And no matter what your users' level of expertise is, if you force them to check their restrictions, you should educate them properly so they know when they must check their restrictions, how they should do so, and what to do when they're approaching the limit.

NETWORK RESTRICTIONS

How to Force Users to Check their Space Usage Periodically

The following sequence of commands can be used in the system login script to force users to check their space restrictions at least monthly:

```
IF DAY="day" THEN BEGIN
     WRITE "It's time to check your disk restrictions. You will be shown"
     WRITE "some statistics about your file server's disk volumes. The"
     WRITE "fourth line shows how much disk space you have left."
     PAUSE
     CHKVOL *
     PAUSE
END
```

(Substitute the desired number—01, 12, 28, etc.—for "day" in the IF...THEN command that begins the above sequence)

Always include this command sequence at the END of a login script, because once the external program execution command (#CHKVOL) is executed, the rest of the login script will be skipped over.

The command sequence given above can be modified to suit your needs. You can include any message in the WRITE commands; you can also have users check weekly, if you want. To do so, just substitute this line for the first line given above:

```
IF DAY_OF_WEEK="day" THEN BEGIN
```

(Substitute the desired day—Monday, Wednesday, Thursday, etc.—for "day" in the above command)

NETWORK USER'S GUIDE

THE NETWARE 286 MANUAL MAKER

> Template for Approach #3 (Disk and Volume Restrictions)
>
> Here is the template to include in your user manuals. If you use it, you may want to move it from this chapter to the section in Chapter 2 titled "What You See When You Log In."

On our network, the amount of disk space you can use has been restricted. If you reach your space limits, you will have to delete some of your old files before you can save files or run some programs again.

So that you don't run into problems, you will be forced to check your space restrictions periodically. When you log in on <list the day of the month or day of the week you used in the IF...THEN statement in the user's login script>, you'll see this message:

<Include the message from the WRITE command in the login script here>

Then the CHKVOL utility, that is used to check your restrictions, is automatically executed.

If you are approaching your limit, take a minute to clean up your directories. List your files, and delete those that you no longer need. You may find the following commands useful as you do this.

NETWORK RESTRICTIONS

Command	Purpose
NDIR REV SORT UPDATE	Sorts files from most- to least-recently updated, making it easy to see which files are old
NDIR REV SORT ACCESS	Sorts files from most- to least-recently accessed, making it easy to see which files you've looked at recently
NDIR SORT SIZE	Sorts files from smallest to largest, making it easy to see what is taking up the most space

Conclusion

The following sample conclusion and transition is based on the generic information in this chapter. If you include it, modify it according to how you modified the chapter and what you plan to cover next.

In this chapter, you learned about your network login and disk restrictions. These included:

1) The restrictions that control when, where, and how you log in.

2) Restrictions on how much disk space you can use on the file server.

In the next chapter, you will learn how to work with directories and files. You will also learn about network security restrictions.

NETWORK USER'S GUIDE

HOW TO USE CHAPTERS 4 AND 5

Working With Directories and Files

Chapters 4 and 5 explain how to work with directories and files. They cover basically the same ground. The difference is that Chapter 4 explains how to complete tasks with the NetWare Command Line utilities, while Chapter 5 explains how to complete tasks with the NetWare Menu utilities.

Since a few tasks can only be done at the command line or with menus, consider your users and their needs before turning to the appropriate chapter.

Generally, the Command Line utilities are best for experienced users who perform a particular task often, and prefer speed and flexibility; the Menu utilities are best for novice users or those who perform a particular task infrequently, and need to be guided along. You may want to skim quickly through the chapters to get an idea of which provides the best approach for the tasks you are going to teach your users about.

Of course, you need not stick strictly with one chapter or the other. You may want to combine material from each to create your own chapter.

CHAPTER OVERVIEW

Working With Directories and Files (Command Line Utilities Version)

The text for this boilerplate chapter is found in
FILESCLU.WP (WordPerfect version)
FILESCLU.ASC (ASCII version)

80	**Directory Structures**
	Explains directory structures, directory paths, and directory names.

83	**Netware Security**
	Choose one of the three approaches:
	84 Basic
	89 Intermediate
	97 Advanced

110	**Drive and Search Drive Mappings**
	Explains drive and search drive mappings.

115	**Working with Files**
	Explains the basics of working with files.

125	**Working with Directories**
	Explains the basics of working with directories

CHAPTER 4

Working with Directories and Files

Command Line Utilities Version

> This chapter explains how to work with directories and files. It explains concepts, such as how directory structures and drive mappings work; and how to complete basic tasks, such as creating directories, copying files, and deleting files.
>
> As with the rest of the Manual Maker, the approach you take in this chapter depends on how you have set up your network, how experienced your users are, and how much you want to teach them.

THE NETWARE 286 MANUAL MAKER

Directory Structures

> This section explains directory structures and how they work.

A network contains a lot of information. Without some sort of organization, that information is very difficult to work with. But rest assured, there is an effective way to organize network information.

The information on a file server's hard disk is organized by the file server's **directory structure**, a type of electronic filing system. A directory structure is made up of **directories**, areas of the hard disk that contain files and other directories. Directories are placed inside other directories, forming a branching, tree-like structure. (In fact, directory structures are often called **directory trees**.) Files are then organized by placing them inside the directory structure.

Directories have special names that describe their relationship to each other in the structure:

A **volume**, the highest level in the structure, is an actual physical area on the hard disk. All directories are subdivisions of the volume.

The **root directory** is the volume level. The root directory is designated by a backslash (\). It contains all of the other directories on the volume.

A directory's **parent directory** is the directory immediately above the directory.

The **current**, or **default**, directory is your current location in the directory structure. NetWare and DOS both look for data and program files in this directory first. If another directory isn't specified, this directory is assumed.

A **subdirectory** of a directory is any directory located below that directory.

80 NETWORK USER'S GUIDE

WORKING WITH DIRECTORIES AND FILES

A Sample Directory Structure

Here is part of a sample directory structure. The levels in this structure are labeled in parentheses at the bottom of the diagram.

> If you want to substitute an actual directory structure from your server, go ahead. I used this one because it corresponds closely to how many users' home directories are set up.
>
> If you use an actual directory structure in this example, use the same directory structure in the next example too.

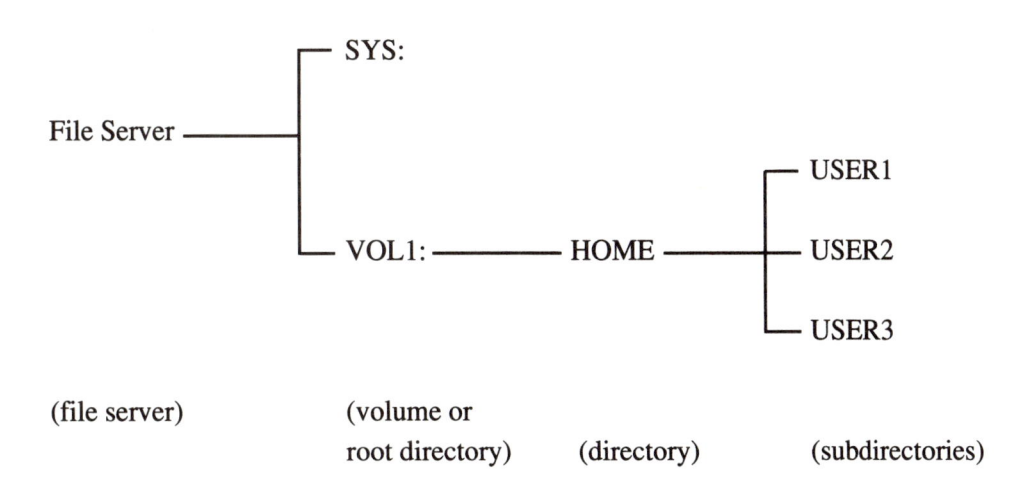

```
                    ┌─ SYS:
File Server ────────┤                              ┌─ USER1
                    └─ VOL1: ──────── HOME ────────┼─ USER2
                                                   └─ USER3
```

(file server)   (volume or   (directory)   (subdirectories)
                     root directory)

NETWORK USER'S GUIDE   81

THE NETWARE 286 MANUAL MAKER

Directory Paths

> This section explains directory paths and directory names.

To find a file, you must know where it is located in the directory structure. A file's location is indicated by its **directory path**, or "path" for short. The path consists of the file server, volume, root directory, and any other directories leading up to the file.

Here is the same directory structure you saw before, with a directory path indicated by asterisks.

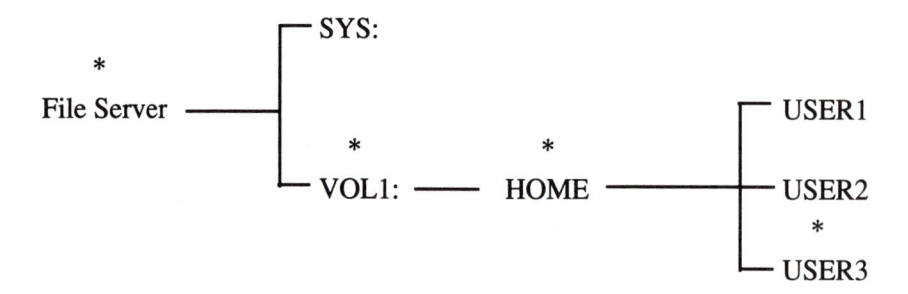

```
                         ┌─ SYS:
      *                  │
   File Server ──────────┤                                    ┌─ USER1
                         │          *              *          │
                         │                                    │
                         └─ VOL1: ──── HOME ──────────────────┤─ USER2
                                                              │    *
                                                              │
                                                              └─ USER3
```

The path indicated by the asterisks would be specified as follows:

FILESERVER\VOL1:HOME\USER3

WORKING WITH DIRECTORIES AND FILES

NetWare Security

You can move around the file server's directory structure freely. But this doesn't mean you can do anything you like anywhere on the file server.

The information on the file server is well-protected by NetWare security. This security determines what directories and files you can access on our network, and what you can do with those directories and files.

Approaches to NetWare Security

Network security is a fairly complex topic, and there are many possible approaches to it. In this section, I have provided three approaches. I recommend that you skim through all the explanations before deciding which approach to take. Then pick the one that comes closest to what you want, and modify it as desired.

NETWORK USER'S GUIDE   83

THE NETWARE 286 MANUAL MAKER

Network Security, Approach #1: Basic

This approach allows you to skirt the issue of security almost entirely. Simply tell users where they can work and what they can do. It is a bottom-line approach that doesn't deal with the actual details of security, but simply explains the end results from a user's perspective. I recommend this approach for novice users.

If you choose this approach,

- Set up your security very carefully so that users won't run into problems.

- Test your security by logging in as the user and making sure that you can do everything you want the user to be able to do.

- Realize that the burden of troubleshooting security-related problems (that account for many common network problems) rests squarely on you, as Supervisor.

WORKING WITH DIRECTORIES AND FILES

Here are the directories you can work with on our network and what you can do in each directory.

> List the directories where users have security privileges (rights), and indicate what the user can do in each directory, based on what his or her rights are. You can do this as follows:
>
> 1. Log in as the user.
>
> 2. Move to a directory where the user has the Create right.
>
> 3. At the DOS prompt, type WHOAMI /R >MYRIGHTS
>
> 4. Now retrieve the file MYRIGHTS into this document and remove any extraneous information.
>
> 5. Delete the file MYRIGHTS from the directory where you created it.

> If you customize the preceding example, you should also explain it. The following example walks you through the process of customizing the example for user Diana, and gives you ideas and sample explanations. (Because the example is lengthy, I haven't put it into comments. You will want to delete most of this explanation from your user manuals, of course. However, you may want to modify portions of it for use in your manuals.)

NETWORK USER'S GUIDE   85

THE NETWARE 286 MANUAL MAKER

Example: Customizing the Security Section

To modify this section for user Diana, complete these steps.

1. Log in as Diana.

2. Move to Diana's personal directory, SYS:HOME\DIANA.

3. Type CLS.

4. Type WHOAMI /R >MYRIGHTS

5. Move to the appropriate place in this document.

6. Retrieve the file MYRIGHTS into this document (SHIFT F10, \HOME\DIANA\MYRIGHTS).

At this point, MYRIGHTS will look similar to the following:

^^ ^P ^–^Q ^^ ^P ^– ^Q ^^You are user DIANA attached to server
LATE, connection 3.
Server LATE is running NetWare 286 V2.15 Rev. C.
Login time: Thursday July 5, 1990 1:54 pm
 [R O S] SYS:LOGIN
 [R O S] SYS:PUBLIC
   [RWCO SM] SYS:MAIL/B00001B
 [RWCODPSM] SYS:DIANA
   [R O S] SYS:MENU
 [R O S] SYS:WP51

WORKING WITH DIRECTORIES AND FILES

7. Remove the extraneous characters and fix the spacing so that MYRIGHTS looks like this:

   ```
   [R    O  S   ] SYS:LOGIN
   [R    O  S   ] SYS:PUBLIC
   [RWCO    SM ]] SYS:MAIL/B00001B
   [RWCODPSM] SYS:DIANA
   [R    O  S   ] SYS:MENU
   [R    O  S   ] SYS:WP51
   ```

8. Add explanations.

You may want to comment on how and why the tree is organized this way. For example,

   A. Give a general explanation of each directory's purpose. (You may want to delete the directories that you don't want to tell the user about—for example most users don't need to know about directories such as SYS:LOGIN, SYS:PUBLIC, and SYS:MAIL.)

   B. Mention which directories contain applications and utilities, and which contain data files.

   C. Point out the user's home directory, if you have created one.

   D. Explain which directories contain shared files, such as database files, and tell who else has access to such directories.

You will also want to tell the user what he or she can do in each directory (create files, look at files, organize a structure beneath, etc.). Use the rights sets as your guide as you do this.

THE NETWARE 286 MANUAL MAKER

The MYRIGHTS file, with explanations, now looks like this:

[RWOCDPSM]   SYS:DIANA   This is your personal directory. You have all security privileges here. You can list, create, delete, and modify files; create, delete, and rename directories; and assign security.

[R O S]   SYS:MENU   This directory contains the files used to run the menus you see when you log in. Your security privileges allow you to run these files, but nothing else.

[R O S]   SYS:WP51   This directory contains the WordPerfect application files. Your security privileges allow you to run these files, but nothing else.

WORKING WITH DIRECTORIES AND FILES

9. Delete the rights sets and adjust the spacing. After this step, the sample file MYRIGHTS looks like this:

SYS:DIANA   This is your personal directory. You have all security privileges here. You can list, create, delete, and modify files; create, delete, and rename directories; and assign security.

SYS:MENU   This directory contains the files used to run the menus you see when you log in. Your security privileges allow you to run these files, but nothing else.

SYS:WP51   This directory contains the WordPerfect application files. Your security privileges allow you to run these files, but nothing else.

Network Security, Approach #2: Intermediate

This approach deals briefly with security, explaining everything that most non-administrative users need to know. It is a middle-of-the-road approach that covers only effective rights and how they determine what a user can do in a directory. I recommend it for most intermediate users.

If you choose this approach, you should still set up and test your security carefully. If security problems do come up, you will probably still have to help users, since they cannot change their own security. But even so, I think it is worth teaching users a little about security, because many common problems are security-related (for example, not being able to run an application or save a file).

THE NETWARE 286 MANUAL MAKER

Your network security is based on the security privileges that you are allowed to exercise in any given directory. These are called your "effective rights." There are eight rights, shown here between brackets:

[RWOCDPSM]

Each letter stands for a right that allows certain privileges, as summarized in the following table.

Letter	Right	Allows you to
R	Read	See the contents of files and execute application files
W	Write	Change the contents of existing files
O	Open	Open files for use
C	Create	Create files and directories
D	Delete	Delete files and directories
P	Parental	Assign security
S	Search	List files in a directory
M	Modify	Change the security attributes of files and directories

WORKING WITH DIRECTORIES AND FILES

Viewing Your Effective Rights Throughout the Directory Tree

To know what your security privileges allow you to do, you need to see your effective rights throughout the directory tree. To do so, type

WHOAMI /R

You see a display similar to the following:

You are user DIANA attached to server LATE, connection 3.
Server LATE is running NetWare 286 V2.15 Rev. C.
Login time: Thursday July 5, 1990 1:54 pm

[R O S] SYS:LOGIN
[R O S] SYS:PUBLIC
[RWCO SM] SYS:MAIL/B00001B
[RWCODPSM] SYS:DIANA
[R O S] SYS:MENU
[R O S] SYS:WP51

NETWORK USER'S GUIDE   91

THE NETWARE 286 MANUAL MAKER

You can customize this section to show exactly what a user will see. Here is how:

1. Log in as the user.

2. Type

   WHOAMI /R > *path:RIGHTS*

   Use a path leading up to a directory where the user has the Create right.

3. Delete the example given here, and delete "similar to this" in the sentence that introduces the example.

4. Retrieve the file RIGHTS into the text here (SHIFT + F10, \DIRTREE).

5. Remove extraneous characters and fix spacing to clean up the text.

If you customize this example, you should also explain it. The following example walks you through the process of customizing the example for user Diana, and gives you ideas and sample explanations. (Because the example is lengthy, I haven't put it into comments. You will want to delete most of this explanation from your users' manuals, of course. However, you may want to modify portions of it for use in your manuals.)

WORKING WITH DIRECTORIES AND FILES

Example: Customizing the Security Section

To modify this security section for user Diana, complete these steps.

1. Log in as Diana.

2. Move to Diana's personal directory, SYS:HOME\DIANA.

3. Type CLS.

4. Type WHOAMI /R >MYRIGHTS.

5. Move to the appropriate place in this document.

6. Retrieve the file MYRIGHTS into this document (SHIFT F10, \HOME\DIANA\MYRIGHTS).

Unmodified, MYRIGHTS looks something like this at this point:

^^ ^P ^–^Q ^^ ^P ^– ^Q ^^You are user DIANA attached to server LATE, connection 3.
Server LATE is running NetWare 286 V2.15 Rev. C.
Login time: Thursday July 5, 1990 1:54 pm
  [R   O   S   ] SYS:LOGIN
  [R   O   S   ] SYS:PUBLIC
  [RWCO SM] SYS:MAIL/B00001B
  [RWCODPSM] SYS:DIANA
  [R   O   S   ] SYS:MENU
  [R   O   S   ] SYS:WP51

THE NETWARE 286 MANUAL MAKER

7. Remove the extraneous characters and fix the spacing so that MYRIGHTS looks like this:

```
[R    O  S  ] SYS:LOGIN
[R    O  S  ] SYS:PUBLIC
[RWCO    SM] SYS:MAIL/B00001B
[RWCODPSM] SYS:DIANA
[R O     S  ] SYS:MENU
[R O     S  ] SYS:WP51
```

8. Add explanations.

You may want to comment on how and why the tree is organized this way. For example,

A. Give a general explanation of each directory's purpose. (You may want to delete the directories that you don't want to tell the user about—for example most users don't need to know about directories such as SYS:LOGIN, SYS:PUBLIC, and SYS:MAIL.)

B. Mention which directories contain applications and utilities, and which contain data files.

C. Point out the user's home directory, if you have created one.

D. Explain which directories contain shared files, such as database files, and tell who else has access to such directories.

You will also want to tell the user what he or she can do in each directory (create files, look at files, organize a structure beneath, etc.). Use the rights sets as your guide as you do this.

WORKING WITH DIRECTORIES AND FILES

The MYRIGHTS file, with explanations, now looks like this:

[R O S   ]   Diana has Read, Open, and Search rights in four directories. Read and Open allows Diana to read the contents of files in the directories where she has this right, and Search allows her to list the files. This combination of rights allows Diana to run executable (program) files. Diana has these rights in the LOGIN directory, that contains the files needed to log in to the network; the PUBLIC directory contains the NetWare utilities and other system files; the MENU directory contains files needed to run custom menus; and the WP51 directory contains word processing application files. Diana has Read, Open, and Search rights in these directories because she needs to run the programs they contain. She doesn't have any other rights because she shouldn't be able to delete, rename, or otherwise modify these files.

[W C   ]   Diana has the Write and Create rights in the MAIL directory. This creates a "drop-box" directory, where Diana can only create files. The files created in this directory have to do with the NetWare electronic mail system.

[RWOCDPSM]   Diana has all rights in her home directory (DIANA), and the directories beneath it (MYM and WORDPROC). Thus, she has all privileges here.

NETWORK USER'S GUIDE   95

THE NETWARE 286 MANUAL MAKER

Checking Your Effective Rights for Individual Directories

You've just learned how to see your effective rights throughout the directory tree. Sometimes, however, you will want to check your effective rights just for your current directory. To do so, type

    RIGHTS

You see a display similar to the following:

```
F:\>rights
FS15/SYS:
Your Effective Rights are [RWOCDPSM]:
    You may Read from Files.                  (R)
    You may Write to Files                    (W)
    You may Open existing Files.              (O)
    You may Create new Files.                 (C)
    You may Make new Subdirectories.          (C)
    You may Delete existing Files.            (D)
    You may Erase existing Subdirectories.    (D)
    You may Change Users' Directory Rights.   (P)
    You may Search the Directory.             (S)
    You may Modify File Status Flags.         (M)

    You have ALL RIGHTS to this directory area.

F:\>
```

96   **NETWORK USER'S GUIDE**

WORKING WITH DIRECTORIES AND FILES

> Network Security, Approach #3: Advanced
>
> This approach offers a complete explanation of security, including effective rights, trustee rights, maximum rights masks, and attributes. I recommend it if you have advanced users who
>
> - You have given the Parental right in some directories and expect them to assign security in those directories
>
> - You want to train to be as independent as possible
>
> - You expect to troubleshoot

NETWORK USER'S GUIDE

THE NETWARE 286 MANUAL MAKER

Your network security is based on the security privileges that you are allowed to exercise in any given directory. These are called your "effective rights." There are eight rights shown here between brackets:

[RWOCDPSM]

Each letter stands for a right that allows certain privileges, as summarized in the following table.

Letter	Right	Allows you to
R	Read	See the contents of files and execute application files
W	Write	Change the contents of existing files
O	Open	Open files for use
C	Create	Create files and directories
D	Delete	Delete files and directories
P	Parental	Assign security
S	Search	List files in a directory
M	Modify	Change the security attributes of files and directories

WORKING WITH DIRECTORIES AND FILES

Viewing Your Effective Rights Throughout the Directory Tree

To know what your security privileges allow you to do, you need to see your effective rights throughout the directory tree. To do so, type

WHOAMI /R

You see a display similar to the following:

You are user DIANA attached to server LATE, connection 3.
Server LATE is running NetWare 286 V2.15 Rev. C.
Login time: Thursday July 5, 1990 1:54 pm

```
            [R   O   S   ] SYS:LOGIN
            [R   O   S   ] SYS:PUBLIC
            [RWCO    SM ] SYS:MAIL/B00001B
            [RWCODPSM] SYS:DIANA
            [R   O   S   ] SYS:MENU
            [R   O   S   ] SYS:WP51
```

NETWORK USER'S GUIDE   99

THE NETWARE 286 MANUAL MAKER

You can customize this section to show exactly what a user sees. Here is how:

1. Log in as the user.

2. Type

   WHOAMI /R > *path*:RIGHTS

   Use a path leading up to a directory where the user has the Create right.

3. Delete the example given here, and delete "similar to this" in the sentence that introduces the example.

4. Retrieve the file RIGHTS into the text here (SHIFT + F10, \DIRTREE).

5. Remove extraneous characters and fix spacing to clean up the text.

If you customize this example, you should also explain it. The following example walks you through the process of customizing the example for user Diana, and gives you ideas and sample explanations. (Because the example is lengthy, I haven't put it into comments. You will want to delete most of this explanation from your users' manuals, of course. However, you may want to modify portions of it for use in your manuals.)

WORKING WITH DIRECTORIES AND FILES

Example: Customizing the Security Section

To modify this security section for user Diana, complete these steps.

1. Log in as Diana.

2. Move to Diana's personal directory, SYS:HOME\DIANA.

3. Type CLS.

4. Type WHOAMI /R >MYRIGHTS

5. Move to the appropriate place in this document.

6. Retrieve the file MYRIGHTS into this document (SHIFT F10, \HOME\DIANA\MYRIGHTS).

Unmodified, MYRIGHTS looks something like this at this point:

```
^^ ^P ^– ^Q ^^ ^P ^– ^Q ^^You are user DIANA attached to server LATE,
connection 3.
Server LATE is running NetWare286 V2.15 Rev. C.
Login time: Thursday  July 5, 1990  1:54 pm
  [ R  O  S ]  SYS:LOGIN
  [ R  O  S ]  SYS:PUBLIC
     [RWCO SM]  SYS:MAIL/B00001B
  [RWCODPSM] SYS:DIANA
     [ R  O  S ]  SYS:MENU
```

NETWORK USER'S GUIDE

THE NETWARE 286 MANUAL MAKER

[R O S] SYS:WP51

7. Remove the extraneous characters and fix the spacing so that MYRIGHTS looks like this:

```
[R    O    S  ] SYS:LOGIN
[R    O    S  ] SYS:PUBLIC
[RWCO      SM] SYS:MAIL/B00001B
[RWCODPSM] SYS:DIANA
[R    O    S  ] SYS:MENU
[R    O    S  ] SYS:WP51
```

8. Add explanations.

You may want to comment on how and why the tree is organized this way. For example,

A. Give a general explanation of each directory's purpose. (You may want to delete the directories that you don't want to tell the user about—for example most users don't need to know about directories such as SYS:LOGIN, SYS:PUBLIC, and SYS:MAIL.)

B. Mention which directories contain applications and utilities, and which contain data files.

C. Point out the user's home directory, if you have created one.

D. Explain which directories contain shared files, such as database files, and tell who else has access to such directories.

You will also want to tell the user what he or she can do in each directory (create files, look at files, organize a structure beneath, etc.). Use the rights sets as your guide as you do this.

WORKING WITH DIRECTORIES AND FILES

The MYRIGHTS file, with explanations, now looks like this:

[R O S]   Diana has Read, Open, and Search rights in four directories. Read and Open allows Diana to read the contents of files in the directories where she has this right, and Search allows her to list the files. This combination of rights allows Diana to run executable (program) files. Diana has these rights in the LOGIN directory that contains the files needed to log in to the network; the PUBLIC directory contains the NetWare utilities and other system files; the MENU directory contains files needed to run custom menus; and the WP51 directory contains word processing application files. Diana has Read, Open, and Search rights in these directories because she needs to run the programs they contain. She doesn't have any other rights because she shouldn't be able to delete, rename, or otherwise modify these files.

[W C]   Diana has the Write and Create rights in the MAIL directory. This creates a "drop-box" directory, where Diana can only create files. The files created in this directory have to do with the NetWare electronic mail system.

[RWOCDPSM]   Diana has all rights in her home directory (DIANA), and the directories beneath it (MYM and WORDPROC). Thus, she has all privileges here.

NETWORK USER'S GUIDE   103

THE NETWARE 286 MANUAL MAKER

Checking Your Effective Rights for Individual Directories

You've just learned how to see your effective rights throughout the directory tree. Sometimes, however, you will want to check your effective rights for just your current directory. To do so, type

    RIGHTS

How Your Effective Rights Were Determined

Your effective rights are the rights you can actually exercise in a directory and are determined by the following:

- The security privileges granted to you as a user ("**trustee rights**")

- The security privileges that a directory allows ("**maximum rights mask**")

To have an effective right in a given directory, your trustee rights for the directory must include the right, and so must the directory's rights mask. If you want to see how your effective rights for a directory were determined, you need to see both your trustee rights for the directory and the directory's maximum rights mask. The next page explains how to do so.

THE NETWARE 286 MANUAL MAKER

To see a directory's maximum rights mask,

1. Go to the directory's parent directory.

2. Type
   LISTDIR /R

You see a display similar to the following:

```
F:\>listdir /r

Sub-directories of FS15/SYS:
   SYSTEM        [RWOCDPSM]
   LOGIN         [RWOCDPSM]
   MAIL          [RWOCDPSM]
   PUBLIC        [RWOCDPSM]
   UTILS         [RWOCDPSM]
   BRIEF         [RWOCDPSM]
6 sub-directories found

F:\>
```

WORKING WITH DIRECTORIES AND FILES

To see the directory's trustees and their rights, go to the directory and type

    TLIST

You see a display similar to the following:

```
F:\>tlist
SYS:
No user trustees.
 —
Group trustees:
  MIS                   [RWOCDPSM]   (The Computer Guys in 351)

F:\>
```

If you are a trustee of the directory, you are listed, along with your trustee rights in that directory.

THE NETWARE 286 MANUAL MAKER

Security Attributes

> In addition to your effective rights, security attributes may affect what you can do with the files in a particular directory.

Security attributes apply to all users, regardless of their effective rights. They are used mainly as a safeguard against mistakes on the part of any user. Here they are, and what they affect.

Read Write/Read Only—Files in directories marked Read Write can be read from and written to; files in directories marked Read Only cannot be changed, only read.

Shareable/Non-Shareable—Files in directories marked Shareable can be opened by more than one user at a time; files in directories marked Non-Shareable can only be opened by one user at a time.

To see the security attributes of a directory's files, go to the directory and type

    FLAG

You see a display similar to the following:

```
F:\>flag

FS15/SYS:
   TEMP1.828      Non-shareable Read/Write
   SKIPLIST.TXT   Non-shareable Read/Write
   FILE16.WP5     Non-shareable Read/Write
   FILE15.WP5     Non-shareable Read/Write
   FILE18.WP5     Non-shareable Read/Write
   FILE19.WP5     Non-shareable Read/Write
   FILE20.WP5     Non-shareable Read/Write
   FILE21.WP5     Non-shareable Read/Write
   SCREEN1.TXT    Non-shareable Read/Write
   SCREEN2.DOC    Non-shareable Read/Write

F:\>
```

NETWORK USER'S GUIDE

WORKING WITH DIRECTORIES AND FILES

Moving Up and Down the Directory Tree

> Explains how to move up and down the levels of the directory tree with the CD command.

Now you are ready to learn how to move around the directory structure. The following table summarizes how to move up and down in the directory structure. Practice using these commands until you feel comfortable with them.

Type ...	To ...
CD ..	Move up one directory level.
CD ...	Move up two directory levels.
CD	Move up three directory levels.
CD *subdirectory*	Move down one directory level. (If you need to see your current directory's subdirectories, type LISTDIR.)
CD *subdirectory\ subdirectory*	Move down two directory levels (from your current directory).

> Customize this section by adding actual directory names to the general instructions given here. You can even delete the general instructions given here and create directions specifically tailored to your directory structure. This would take some effort, but if you have novice users who need a lot of hand-holding, it might be a good idea. On the other hand, if your directory structure will change frequently, it is probably better not to get too specific.

NETWORK USER'S GUIDE

THE NETWARE 286 MANUAL MAKER

Drive Mappings

> Explains drive mappings.

Drive mappings provide another method to move around in the directory structure. Here is how they work.

Drive mappings point to a particular place in a file server's directory structure. A drive letter is assigned ("mapped") to a directory path, like this:

    Drive F: = *SERVER\VOLUME:DIRECTORY*

Use drive mappings to go directly to a specific point in the directory structure. Type the drive letter, followed by a colon, and press ENTER. In the preceding example, you could go to SERVER\VOLUME:DIRECTORY by typing

    F:

Usually, drives are mapped to the areas in the directory structure that you work with most. To see your drive mappings, type

    MAP

WORKING WITH DIRECTORIES AND FILES

The mappings are displayed similar to the following:

Drive A: maps to a local disk.
Drive B: maps to a local disk.
Drive C: maps to a local disk.
Drive D: maps to a local disk.
Drive F: = SERVER\VOLUME: \
Drive G: = SERVER\VOLUME:HOME\CHRIS

SEARCH1: = Z:. [SERVER\VOLUME: \PUBLIC]
SEARCH2: = Y:. [SERVER\VOLUME: \]
SEARCH3: = X:. [SERVER\VOLUME: \WORDPROCESSOR]

To customize the preceding section to show the user's actual drive mappings,

1. Delete the example given in the text here, and delete "similar to this" in the sentence that introduces the example.

2. Log in as the user.

3. Go to a directory where the user has the Create right.

4. Type

    MAP >MAPPINGS

5. Retrieve the file MAPPINGS into the text here (SHIFT + F10, MAPPINGS).

6. Delete extraneous characters and fix spacing as necessary.

THE NETWARE 286 MANUAL MAKER

> If you customize this section to show the user's actual mappings, you should also explain the mappings. Sample text that you can use as a starting point is given next.

Here are your drive mappings and what they mean.

Drive	Maps to
A-E	Your PC's floppy and hard disk drives. NetWare security does not apply to these drives. (You can re-map these drives to network drives if desired.)
F	The root directory of volume <VOLUME NAME>.
G	Your personal (home) directory. This is where you keep your personal files. You have all security privileges here—you may create, delete, and rename files and directories, and assign security here.

> Note that both drive and search drive mappings are shown when mappings are listed. Most users won't really need to know about search drive mappings; if you don't want to teach your users about them, you may want to point out the search drive mappings briefly, just tell users not to worry about them. If you do want to teach your users about search drive mappings, use the material given next.

WORKING WITH DIRECTORIES AND FILES

Search Drive Mappings

> Explains search drive mappings (only necessary for advanced users).

Like drive mappings, search drive mappings point to a location in the file server's directory structure. But search drives work a little differently; they tell the network where to look for a file when it cannot be found in the current directory. The main purpose of search drive mappings is to point to directories that contain executable files (programs you can run), thus preventing you from having to put copies of those files in every directory where you need to work. (Users familiar with DOS recognize that search drives are similar to the PATH command.)

Search drive mappings have both numbers and letters. The numbers begin with one and increase sequentially (2, 3, 4, on up to 16); the letters begin with Z and continue backwards through the alphabet (Y, X, W, and so on).

To see your search drive mappings, type

> MAP

Search drive mappings are shown in the lower half of the display.

NETWORK USER'S GUIDE

THE NETWARE 286 MANUAL MAKER

> At this point, you may want to explain what users' specific search drive mappings are used for.
>
> For example, most users should have a search drive mapping to SYS: PUBLIC, that contains the NetWare utilities. To explain this mapping, you would tell them that this is the search drive mapping that points to where the NetWare utilities are located.
>
> Generally, users also have search drive mappings to directories that contain application files. You can explain these mappings too. If you do, this may be a good place to tell users about the applications they will be using on the network.
>
> Sample text that you can use as a starting point is given next.

Here are your search drive mappings and what they mean.

SEARCH1   The file server's PUBLIC directory, where all the NetWare utilities are located. This search mapping allows you to access the NetWare utilities.

SEARCH2   The file server's <insert the directory name> directory, that contains the <insert a description> files. This search mapping allows you to access <utility files, application files, etc.>. You can <describe what their security privileges allow them to do—usually just run files> in this directory.

WORKING WITH DIRECTORIES AND FILES

Looking at Files

> Vital for most users.

NetWare gives you many powerful options for listing files. You can limit or sort file listings based on a number of different criteria. The following section summarizes some of the most common options for listing and sorting files.

THE NETWARE 286 MANUAL MAKER

Type ...	**To see ...**
DIR	Files and directories; file size and last update; directory creation date and time
DIR /W	Files and directories, listed in columns across the screen
NDIR .	Files, file size, last modified date and time, attributes, and owners; directories, inherited rights mask, your effective rights in the directory, owner, and creation date and time
NDIR . ACCESS BEF *mm-dd-yy*	Directories and files last accessed before the date specified in the command
NDIR . ACCESS AFT *mm-dd-yy*	Directories and files last accessed after the date specified in the command
NDIR . UPDATE BEF *mm-dd-yy*	Directories and files last updated before the date specified in the command
NDIR . UPDATE AFT *mm-dd-yy*	Directories and files last updated after the date specified in the command
NDIR . OWNER *your username*	Files and directories that you have created
NDIR . SORT SIZE	Files sorted by size, smallest to largest
NDIR . SORT ACCESS	Files sorted based on last access date, earliest to latest
NDIR . SORT UPDATE	Files sorted based on last update, earliest to latest

WORKING WITH DIRECTORIES AND FILES

Copying Files

Files can be copied with the DOS COPY or the NetWare NCOPY command. The following section summarizes some of the most common variations of the NCOPY command.

> The following instructions assume that users know what source and target directories are, and how to use wildcards. If you have novice users who don't, you may want to include the following explanation.
>
> Here is an explanation of some terms used in the following instructions:
>
> **Source directory**—the directory you are copying a file from
>
> **Target directory**—the directory you are copying a file to
>
> **Wildcards**—an asterisk (*) that can be used to substitute for other characters in a filename. For example, you can specify all files beginning with "F" by typing
>
> F*

THE NETWARE 286 MANUAL MAKER

Type ...	To...
NCOPY *filename target directory*	Copy a file from your current directory to another directory
NCOPY *.* *target directory*	Copy all the files in your current directory to another directory. For example, to copy all the files from floppy disk A, type NCOPY A:*.* *target directory*
NCOPY pattern*.* *target directory*	Copy only files that match the pattern from your current directory to another directory. For example, to copy all the files beginning with F, type NCOPY f*.* *target directory*

If your users have existing files on floppy diskettes, right now might be a good time to have them copy those files from the diskettes to the network.

On the other hand, if you expect your users to create their own directory structures, you may want to wait until after they have done so before they copy their files to the network.

WORKING WITH DIRECTORIES AND FILES

Deleting and Renaming Files

From time to time, you need to "clean up" and reorganize your files. That is when you will want to know how to delete and rename them. The DOS DEL, ERASE, and REN commands are used to do this.

Type...	**To ...**
DEL *filename* or ERASE *filename*	Delete a file in your current directory
DEL *path:filename* or ERASE *path:filename*	Delete a file that is not in your current directory
REN *filename newname*	Rename a file in your current directory
REN *path:filename newname*	Rename a file that is not in your current directory

THE NETWARE 286 MANUAL MAKER

Backing Up and Restoring Files

> You may want to substitute a short explanation of your backup policy for the generic paragraph below. If you have diskless workstations or don't require users to back up their files, delete this section.

Even though we back up network files regularly, you should still back up your personal files as a precaution. You needn't back up all your files every day; just back up the ones you have modified that day.

> Explain the best method to back up files on your system. For most users, the simplest thing to do is to back up to a floppy diskette, as explained here.
>
> But if you have users on diskless workstations, or if you are concerned about confidential information floating around on floppy diskettes, you may want to have them back up to another medium.

To back up a file, copy it to a floppy diskette by typing

NCOPY *filename targetpath*

Then, should you need to restore from the backup, you can do so by copying the backup file to its original location.

WORKING WITH DIRECTORIES AND FILES

Salvaging Files

> I recommend that you teach users how to salvage files. They won't always be able to do so, but when they can, it saves them a lot of anxiety.

If you delete a file accidentally and realize your mistake quickly enough, you may be able to recover the file with the SALVAGE utility. SALVAGE works as long as you use it immediately after you delete the file.

To salvage a file, type

    SALVAGE

All salvageable files are recovered, and a list of the salvaged files is displayed on the screen.

> If you use WordPerfect, PlanPerfect, or P-Edit on your network, you might want to note the following. All of these applications create temporary files that are deleted when you exit the application. Since SALVAGE only recovers the file(s) deleted with the last DELETE or ERASE command, if you delete a file accidentally and exit the application to salvage the file, you will only salvage the temporary files that were deleted when you exited the application. Instead of exiting the application, use CTRL-F1 to go to DOS and run SALVAGE.

THE NETWARE 286 MANUAL MAKER

Printing Files

> If you use a third-party printing program on your network, you will want to substitute instructions for using that printing program for the NetWare printing instructions given here.

> Generally, I don't recommend that you teach users the details of how NetWare printing works, or how to print their files with the NetWare command line interface. This is why.
>
> - For most users, it is much easier to print using applications. If you set up network printing properly and test it thoroughly, printing from applications should be transparent to users.
>
> - NetWare printing is complex, and users need to understand it fairly well to be comfortable with the NetWare printing utilities. Generally, it makes more sense to set up custom menus for users to print from than to educate users about the many printing parameters.
>
> - If users need to print with CAPTURE, it makes more sense to include the CAPTURE TI=*n* command in their login scripts or a batch file than to try to teach them how CAPTURE works (see the explanation of CAPTURE in Chapter 6, "Command Line Utilities Reference").

> However, if you do want to teach your users how to print from the command line, you can include this short explanation of NetWare printing and the NPRINT command in their manuals.

WORKING WITH DIRECTORIES AND FILES

Printing on a network is a little more involved than printing with a regular personal computer. Instead of going directly from your personal computer to the printer, print data must follow a somewhat more complex path. This path was set up when the network was installed, so you shouldn't have to worry about it. But briefly, it is as follows.

First, the print data ("print job" in NetWare terms) goes to a network print queue, located on the file server's hard disk. Like the personal computer's buffer or spool area, the print queue is a waiting area for print jobs that pile up faster than they can be printed. However, a network print queue can have multiple print queues and each can store jobs from many different users. Which queue your print jobs go to depends on how network printing has been set up, or which queue you specify when you print the job.

> You may want to tell them which print queue(s) their print jobs will go to, and why, here.

A process within the NetWare operating system, called a print server, takes print jobs out of the queue and sends them to the printer. As with print queues, print servers are established when network printing is set up. Which queues a print server services, and which printers it sends print jobs to, depends on how network printing was set up.

> You may want to tell them which printer(s) their print jobs will go to, and why, here.

THE NETWARE 286 MANUAL MAKER

Luckily, you don't really need to know all this information to print a file. If the file was created in a network application or text editor, just print it from there. If the file was created in a non-network application or text editor, you can print it with NPRINT. The following section summarizes how this is done.

Type ...	**To ...**
NPRINT *filename*	Print a file created in a non-network application or text editor
NPRINT *filename* NOTIFY	Be notified when the job has printed
NPRINT *filename* C=*n*	Print a certain number of copies (replace *n* with the desired number)

WORKING WITH DIRECTORIES AND FILES

Working with Directories

Most of the time, when you clean up and reorganize, you will be working with files. But sometimes you will also want to work with the directory structure itself.

The following section summarizes how to list, create, rename, and delete directories, as well as how to copy directory structures.

Type ...	**To ...**
LISTDIR	List your current directory's subdirectories
MD *directory*	Create a subdirectory beneath your current directory
RENDIR *directory newname*	Rename a subdirectory of your current directory
RD *directory*	Delete a subdirectory of your current directory (the subdirectory must be completely empty before you can delete it)

NETWORK USER'S GUIDE 125

THE NETWARE 286 MANUAL MAKER

Ideas for Creating Your Own Directory Structures

> Include if user
>
> - Is sophisticated enough to organize his or her files in directories
>
> - Has Parental and Create rights at any point in the directory structure (necessary to create directories)

The directory structure for the file server organizes files for everyone who works on the file server. In the areas where you keep your own personal files, you may want to create your own limited directory structures to organize your files. In fact, if you have more than a few files, this is a good idea; you shouldn't dump your electronic files onto a computer without organizing them any more than you would dump your paper files onto a desk or into a drawer.

As you plan your directory structure, consider these questions.

1. What will I organize my files based on?

Consider what files you have to manage, and what kind of a structure would help you best organize them. It may be useful to think of how you would organize ordinary paper files efficiently, and use that as a guideline for planning your directory structure.

2. Will other people need to access my files?

If so, it may make sense to put files that need to be accessed by the same people in the same directories.

WORKING WITH DIRECTORIES AND FILES

3. What should I name my directories?

Give your directories meaningful, descriptive names.

4. How many levels deep should I make my directory structure?

Generally, it is best not to make the directory structure more than 3-4 levels deep.

If you start getting a lot of files in a directory, consider subdividing the directory and reorganizing your files.

Once you have decided how you want to organize your personal directory structures, use the DOS MD command to create directories according to your plan.

THE NETWARE 286 MANUAL MAKER

Creating a Directory

To create a directory,

1. Move to the directory that you would like to create the new directory beneath.

2. Type

    MD *directory*

Substitute the name of your new directory for *directory*. Remember, it can only be eight characters long; if you type a longer name, it will be truncated to eight characters.

WORKING WITH DIRECTORIES AND FILES

Setting Up Drive Mappings

> Most users probably won't need to set up drive mappings, and even fewer need to set up search drive mappings. The main reason to set up a search drive mapping is if the user uses personal applications on the network.
>
> In addition, drive and search drive mappings consume directory entries. If you are concerned about excessive drive mappings consuming directory entries, you may not want to teach your users how to set up mappings.
>
> Also, if you didn't include the previous sections explaining drive and search drive mappings, you won't want to include this section either.

You probably won't need to set up drive mappings to your newly-created subdirectories unless your subdirectory structure is quite deep and complex. In most cases, it is easier to use your existing drive mappings to get to the general area, then move up and down the directory structure. But if you do want to set up drive mappings, here is how to do it.

Type

MAP *driveletter:=path*

Substitute the next available letter for driveletter; substitute the desired directory path for *path*. If you need to see which drive letter is the next one available, type MAP to check your existing drive mappings.

NETWORK USER'S GUIDE

THE NETWARE 286 MANUAL MAKER

Saving Mappings in Login Scripts

> This section explains how to save mappings in personal login scripts. Include it only if you want to teach users about their login scripts. Also, if you teach users how to save drive mappings in their login scripts, caution them not to inadvertently override the mappings contained in the system-wide login script.

Drive mappings set up at the command line last only until you log out. Most of the time, you will want your drive mappings to be more permanent than that. To have your drive mappings set up every time you log in, you must save them in your login script.

To do so, complete the following steps:

1. Access the SYSCON utility.

2. Choose "User Information."

3. Choose your name.

4. Choose Login Script.

You will see your login script. It may have many or few commands, depending on how your supervisor has set it up. Be very careful when you are working in the login script. Make sure you understand the intent of each line before you make any changes.

WORKING WITH DIRECTORIES AND FILES

5. To set the drive mapping, type

   MAP *n:=*directory path*

The "*n*" maps the directory to the next available network drive.

6. Exit SYSCON, saving your changes.

Now log in again. Type MAP to display your drive mappings (if they aren't shown when you log in). You should see the drive mapping(s) you added.

THE NETWARE 286 MANUAL MAKER

Setting Security

> Setting security is a fairly advanced topic that most users won't really be concerned with. If you have set up the high-level directory structure properly, users shouldn't have to worry about other users accessing their personal files. Some users may create files in their personal directories that they share with other users; these are probably the only users who might be concerned with setting security.
>
> Remember, unless you have given a user the Parental right in a directory, he or she cannot set security anyway. So you will want to skip this section in manuals you create for users who don't have Parental rights anywhere.
>
> Also, if you include this section, make sure you included the full explanation of security previously, since users need to understand maximum rights masks and trustee rights before they set security.

In the directories where you have the Parental right, you can set security if you want. Unless you will create directories or files that you need to share with other users, you probably won't need to do this, however.

If you do need to assign security, follow these steps.

1. Decide which users need which rights in your directories.

You may want to sketch the directory tree and write in the names of users who need access to certain directories, along with what rights they should be given. Remember, once you have granted a trustee right in a directory, the right trickles down the tree. So you may not need to actually make trustee assignments in every single directory where you want the user to have security privileges.

WORKING WITH DIRECTORIES AND FILES

You may also want to refer to the following rights table as you decide what rights to grant.

Letter	Right	Allows you to
R	Read	See the contents of files and execute application files
W	Write	Change the contents of existing files
O	Open	Open files for use
C	Create	Create files and directories
D	Delete	Delete files and directories
P	Parental	Assign security
S	Search	List files in a directory
M	Modify	Change the security attributes of files and directories

2. Decide if you want to limit the rights that can be exercised in any given directory.

Sometimes, you will want to be sure that a certain right cannot be exercised in a given directory. For example, you may want to make sure that no one can delete files in a given directory. When this is the case, set the directory's maximum rights mask so the directory does not allow the right to be exercised. For example, if you didn't

NETWORK USER'S GUIDE   **133**

THE NETWARE 286 MANUAL MAKER

want anyone to be able to delete files in a directory, you would remove the Delete right from the directory's maximum rights mask. You must do this for each directory, since a maximum rights mask masks rights only for one directory.

If you sketched the directory tree, write in the maximum rights masks on your sketch.

3. Check to be sure that the trustee assignments and maximum rights masks that you have planned gives users the rights you want them to have in your directories.

4. Make trustee assignments.

For each directory where you want to make a trustee assignment, go to the directory and type

> GRANT *rights* TO *username*

Replace *rights* with the abbreviations for the desired rights, with a space between each right; replace *username* with the name of the user you're giving the rights to.

For example, to grant user Mark the Read, Open, and Search rights in a directory, you would go to that directory and type

> GRANT R O S TO MARK

Complete the above steps for every trustee assignment you want to make. Remember that trustee rights filter down through the directory structure, so you need not make a trustee assignment in every directory where you want a user to have rights.

WORKING WITH DIRECTORIES AND FILES

5. Change maximum rights masks if necessary.

    A. Access FILER.

    B. Choose "Current Directory Information."

    C. Choose "Maximum Rights Mask."

    D. To delete a right from the mask, highlight the right, press DELETE, and answer "Yes."

    E. To add a right to the mask, press INSERT and choose the right.

THE NETWARE 286 MANUAL MAKER

Conclusion

The following generic conclusion is based on the unmodified Manual Maker text for this chapter. Modify it based on how you modified the chapter.

In this chapter, you learned about

- Directory structures, directory paths, and directory names

- NetWare security and how it controls what you can do on the network

- Moving around the directory structure with the CD command and drive mappings

- Working with files, including listing, copying, deleting, renaming, backing up and restoring, printing, salvaging, and purging

- Working with directories, including listing, creating, copying, deleting, and renaming

- Setting up your own drive mappings

- Establishing security in your personal areas of the directory structure

CHAPTER OVERVIEW

Working with Directories and Files (Menu Utilities Version)

This boilerplate chapter is found in
FILESMEN.WP (WordPerfect version)
FILESMEN.ASC (ASCII version)

142	**Directory Structures**
	Explains directory structures, directory paths, and directory names.
146	**Drive and Search Drive Mappings**
148	**Netware Security**
	Choose one of the three approaches:
	149 Basic
	154 Intermediate
	160 Advanced
163	**Working with Files**
169	**Working with Directories**
	Explains the basics of working with directories
173	**Setting Up Drive Mappings and Security**

139

CHAPTER 5

Working with Directories and Files

Menu Utilities Version

> This chapter explains how to work with directories and files. It explains concepts, such as directory structures and drive mappings; and how to complete basic tasks, such as creating directories, copying files, and deleting files.
>
> As with the rest of the Manual Maker, the approach you take in this chapter depends on how you have set up your network, how experienced your users are, and how much you want to teach them.

THE NETWARE 286 MANUAL MAKER

Directory Structures

> This section explains directory structures and how they work.

A network contains a lot of information. Without some sort of organization, that information is very difficult to work with. But rest assured, there is an effective way to organize network information.

The information on a file server's hard disk is organized by the file server's **directory structure**, a type of electronic filing system. A directory structure is made up of **directories**, areas of the hard disk that contain files and other directories. Directories are placed inside other directories, forming a branching, tree-like structure. (In fact, directory structures are often called **directory trees**.) Files are then organized by placing them inside the directory structure.

Directories have special names that describe their relationship to each other in the structure:

A **volume**, the highest level in the structure, is an actual physical area on the hard disk. All directories are subdivisions of the volume.

The **root directory** is the volume level. The root directory is designated by a backslash (\). It contains all of the other directories on the volume.

A directory's **parent directory** is the directory immediately above the directory.

The **current**, or **default**, directory is your current location in the directory structure. NetWare and DOS both look for data and program files in this directory first. If another directory isn't specified, this directory is assumed.

A **subdirectory** of a directory is any directory located below that directory.

WORKING WITH DIRECTORIES AND FILES

A Sample Directory Structure

Here is part of a sample directory structure. The levels in this structure are labeled in parentheses at the bottom of the diagram.

> If you want to substitute an actual directory structure from your server, go ahead. I used this one because it corresponds closely to how many users' home directories are set up.
>
> If you use an actual directory structure in this example, use the same directory structure in the next example too.

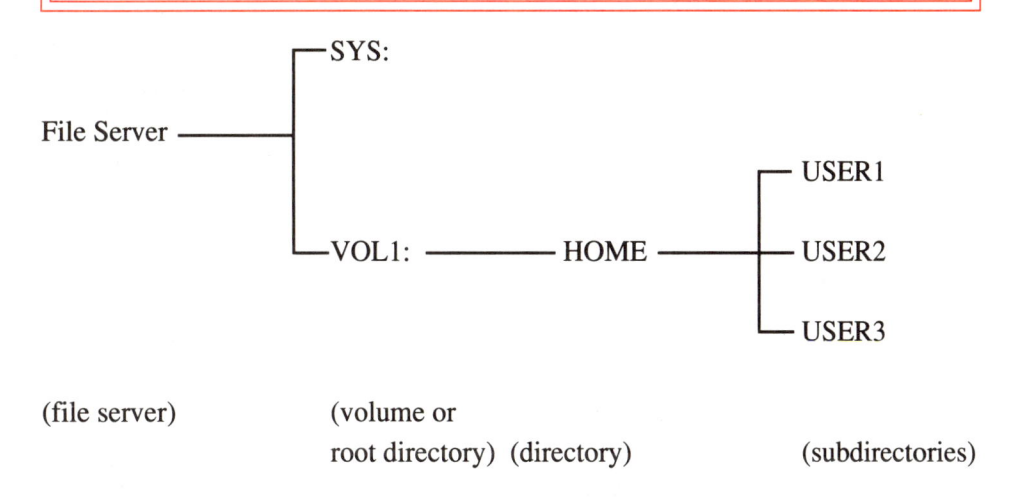

```
                   ┌─ SYS:
File Server ───────┤                              ┌─ USER1
                   └─ VOL1: ──────── HOME ────────┼─ USER2
                                                  └─ USER3

(file server)      (volume or
                   root directory)  (directory)      (subdirectories)
```

NETWORK USER'S GUIDE   143

THE NETWARE 286 MANUAL MAKER

Directory Paths

> This section explains directory paths and directory names.

To find a file, you must know where it is located in the directory structure. A file's location is indicated by its **directory path**, or "path" for short. The path consists of the file server, volume, root directory, and any other directories leading up to the file.

Here is the same directory structure you saw before, with a directory path indicated by asterisks.

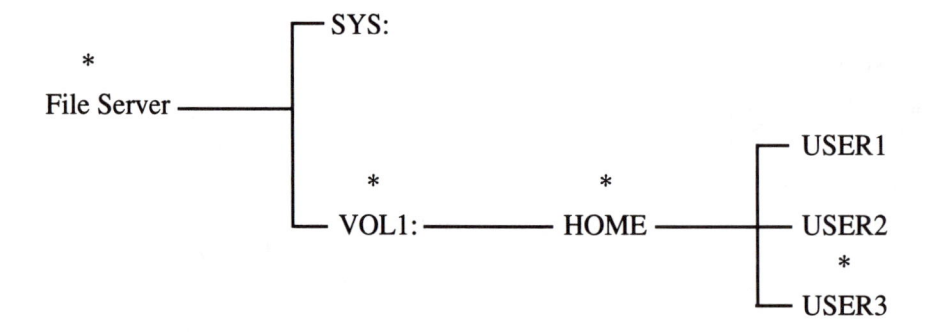

```
                         ┌─ SYS:
    *                    │
File Server ─────────────┤
                         │                              ┌─ USER1
                         │    *              *          │
                         └─ VOL1: ───────── HOME ───────┤── USER2
                                                        │    *
                                                        └─ USER3
```

The path indicated by the asterisks would be specified as follows:

FILESERVER\VOL1:HOME\USER3

144   NETWORK USER'S GUIDE

WORKING WITH DIRECTORIES AND FILES

Exploring the Directory Tree

Now that you understand what directory structures are and how they work, let's move around the directory tree. To do so, complete these steps.

1. Access FILER.

2. Choose "Select Current Directory."

   In the box that appears, you see the directory path for your current directory. It looks something like this:

   FILESERVER/VOLUME:DIRECTORY

3. To move UP a level or levels, use the BACKSPACE key to delete parts of the path. In the example on the preceding page, you could move up to the volume level by deleting the directory so the path looked like this:

   FILESERVER/VOLUME:

   You can also move up a level by choosing the ".." option to go to the directory's parent directory.

4. To move DOWN a level, type the desired path, or press INSERT to list the directory's subdirectories; then choose the directory you want.

   When you have specified the path you want, press ESCAPE, then ENTER. The center of the header now shows the new directory path, that is now your current directory.

NETWORK USER'S GUIDE   145

THE NETWARE 286 MANUAL MAKER

Drive Mappings

> Explains drive mappings.

Drive mappings provide another method to move around in the directory structure. Here is how they work.

Drive mappings point to a particular place in a file server's directory structure. A drive letter is assigned ("mapped") to a directory path, like this:

Drive F: = *SERVER\VOLUME:DIRECTORY*

Usually, drives are mapped to the areas in the directory structure that you work with most. To see your drive mappings,

1. Access SESSION.

2. Choose "Drive Mappings" and your drive mappings are listed.

You probably recognize the directories shown in your mappings; they are most likely the same directories you've just been exploring.

Use drive mappings to go directly to a specific point in the directory structure. To move directly to a directory mapped to a given drive,

3. Press ESCAPE to return to the SESSION "Available Topics" menu.

4. Choose "Select Default Drive."

5. Choose the drive you want to be your current (default) drive. The directory it is mapped to becomes your current directory.

WORKING WITH DIRECTORIES AND FILES

Search Drive Mappings

> Explains search drive mappings (only necessary for advanced users).

Like drive mappings, search drive mappings point to a location in the file server's directory structure. But search drives work a little differently; they tell the network where to look for a file when it cannot be found in the current directory. The main purpose of search drive mappings is to point to directories that contain executable files (programs you can run), thus preventing you from having to put copies of those files in every directory where you need to work. (Users familiar with DOS recognize that search drives are similar to the PATH command.)

Search drive mappings have both numbers and letters. The numbers begin with one and increase sequentially (2, 3, 4, on up to 16); the letters begin with Z and continue backwards through the alphabet (Y, X, W, and so on).

To see your search drive mappings,

1. Access SESSION.

2. Choose "Search Mappings" and your search drive mappings are listed.

NETWORK USER'S GUIDE   147

THE NETWARE 286 MANUAL MAKER

NetWare Security

You can move around the file server's directory structure freely. But this doesn't mean you can do anything you like anywhere on the file server.

The information on the file server is well-protected by NetWare security. This security determines what directories and files you can access on our network, and what you can do with those directories and files.

> Approaches to NetWare Security
>
> Network security is a fairly complex topic, and there are many possible approaches to it.. In this section, I have provided three approaches. I recommend that you skim through all the explanations before deciding which approach to take. Then pick the one that comes closest to what you want, and modify it as desired.

WORKING WITH DIRECTORIES AND FILES

Network Security, Approach #1: Basic

This approach allows you to skirt the issue of security almost entirely. Simply tell users where they can work and what they can do. It is a bottom-line approach that doesn't deal with the actual details of security, but simply explains the end results from a user's perspective. I recommend this approach for novice users.

If you choose this approach,

- Set up your security very carefully so that users won't run into problems.

- Test your security by logging in as the user and making sure that you can do everything you want the user to be able to do.

- Realize that the burden of troubleshooting security- related problems (that account for many common network problems) rests squarely on you, as Supervisor.

THE NETWARE 286 MANUAL MAKER

Here are the directories you can work with on our network and what you can do in each directory.

> List the directories where users have security privileges (rights), and indicate what the user can do in each directory, based on what his or her rights are. You can do this as follows:
>
> 1. Log in as the user.
>
> 2. Move to a directory where the user has the Create right.
>
> 3. At the DOS prompt, type WHOAMI /R >MYRIGHTS
>
> 4. Now retrieve the file MYRIGHTS into this document and remove any extraneous information.
>
> 5. Delete the file MYRIGHTS from the directory where you created it.

> If you customize the preceding example, you should also explain it. The following example walks you through the process of customizing the example for user Diana, and gives you ideas and sample explanations. (Because the example is lengthy, I haven't put it into comments. You will want to delete most of this explanation from your user manuals, of course. However, you may want to modify portions of it for use in your manuals.)

To modify this section for user Diana, complete these steps.

1. Log in as Diana.

2. Move to Diana's personal directory, SYS:HOME\DIANA.

WORKING WITH DIRECTORIES AND FILES

3. Type CLS.

4. Type WHOAMI /R >MYRIGHTS
5. Move to the appropriate place in this document.

6. Retrieve the file MYRIGHTS into this document (SHIFT F10, \HOME\DIANA\MYRIGHTS).

   At this point, MYRIGHTS will look similar to the following:

^^ ^P ^_ ^Q ^^ ^P ^_ ^Q ^^You are user DIANA attached to server LATE, connection 3.
Server LATE is running NetWare 286 V2.15 Rev. C.
Login time: Thursday July 5, 1990 1:54 pm
 [R   O   S] SYS:LOGIN
 [R   O   S] SYS:PUBLIC
     [RWCO SM] SYS:MAIL/B00001B
 [RWCODPSM] SYS:DIANA
     [R   O   S] SYS:MENU
 [R   O   S] SYS:WP51

7. Remove the extraneous characters and fix the spacing so that MYRIGHTS looks like this:

[R   O   S] SYS:LOGIN
[R   O   S] SYS:PUBLIC
[RWCO SM] SYS:MAIL/B00001B
[RWCODPSM] SYS:DIANA
[R   O   S] SYS:MENU
[R   O   S] SYS:WP51

THE NETWARE 286 MANUAL MAKER

    8.   Add explanations.

You may want to comment on how and why the tree is organized this way. For example,

    A. Give a general explanation of each directory's purpose. (You may want to delete the directories that you don't want to tell the user about—for example most users don't need to know about directories such as SYS:LOGIN, SYS:PUBLIC, and SYS:MAIL.)

    B. Mention which directories contain applications and utilities, and which contain data files.

    C. Point out the user's home directory, if you have created one.

    D. Explain which directories contain shared files, such as database files, and tell who else has access to such directories.

You will also want to tell the user what he or she can do in each directory (create files, look at files, organize a structure beneath, etc.). Use the rights sets as your guide as you do this.

The MYRIGHTS file, with explanations, now looks like this:

[RWOCDPSM]   SYS:DIANA   This is your personal directory. You have all security privileges here. You can list, create, delete, and modify files; create, delete, and rename directories; and assign security.

WORKING WITH DIRECTORIES AND FILES

[R O S]   SYS:MENU   This directory contains the files used to run the menus you see when you log in. Your security privileges allow you to run these files, but nothing else.

[R O S]   SYS:WP51   This directory contains the WordPerfect application files. Your security privileges allow you to run these files, but nothing else.

   9. Delete the rights sets and adjust the spacing. After this step, the sample file MYRIGHTS looks like this:

SYS:DIANA   This is your personal directory. You have all security privileges here. You can list, create, delete, and modify files; create, delete, and rename directories; and assign security.

SYS:MENU   This directory contains the files used to run the menus you see when you log in. Your security privileges allow you to run these files, but nothing else.

SYS:WP51   This directory contains the WordPerfect application files. Your security privileges allow you to run these files, but nothing else.

NETWORK USER'S GUIDE

THE NETWARE 286 MANUAL MAKER

> Network Security, Approach #2: Intermediate
>
> This approach deals briefly with security, explaining everything that most non-administrative users need to know. It is a middle-of-the-road approach that covers only effective rights and how they determine what a user can do in a directory. I recommend it for most intermediate users.

> If you choose this approach, you should still set up and test your security carefully. If security problems do come up, you will probably still have to help users, since they cannot change their own security. But even so, I think it is worth teaching users a little about security, because many common problems are security-related (for example, not being able to run an application or save a file).

Your network security is based on the security privileges that you are allowed to exercise in any given directory. These are called your "effective rights." There are eight rights, shown here between brackets:

[RWOCDPSM]

WORKING WITH DIRECTORIES AND FILES

Each letter stands for a right that allows certain privileges, as summarized in the following table.

Letter	Right	Allows you to
R	Read	See the contents of files and execute application files
W	Write	Change the contents of existing files
O	Open	Open files for use
C	Create	Create files and directories
D	Delete	Delete files and directories
P	Parental	Assign security
S	Search	List files in a directory
M	Modify	Change the security attributes of files and directories

THE NETWARE 286 MANUAL MAKER

Your Effective Rights

> Unfortunately, no NetWare Menu utility gives a user an overview of his or her effective rights throughout the entire directory structure. A user can see all of his or her trustee assignments (in SYSCON), but effective rights must be reviewed directory by directory (in FILER).

> For this reason, I recommend that you tell users which directories they have rights to work with, and what their effective rights are in those directories. The following example walks you through the process of doing so for user Diana, and gives you ideas and sample explanations. (Because the example is lengthy, I haven't put it into comments. Delete most of this explanation from your user manuals. You may want to modify portions of it for use in your manuals.)

Example: Customizing the Security Section

To modify this security section for user Diana, complete these steps.

1. Log in as Diana.

2. Move to Diana's personal directory, SYS:HOME\DIANA.

3. Type CLS.

4. Type WHOAMI /R >MYRIGHTS.

5. Move to the appropriate place in this document.

6. Retrieve the file MYRIGHTS into this document (SHIFT F10, \HOME\DIANA\MYRIGHTS).

156 NETWORK USER'S GUIDE

WORKING WITH DIRECTORIES AND FILES

Unmodified, MYRIGHTS looks something like this at this point:

^^ ^P ^_ ^Q ^^ ^P ^_ ^Q ^^You are user DIANA attached to server LATE, connection 3.
Server LATE is running NetWare 386 V3.00 Rev. A.
Login time: Thursday July 5, 1990 1:54 pm
 [R O S] SYS:LOGIN
 [R O S] SYS:PUBLIC
   [RWCO SM] SYS:MAIL/B00001B
 [RWCODPSM] SYS:DIANA
   [R O S] SYS:MENU
 [R O S] SYS:WP51

7. Remove the extraneous characters and fix the spacing so that MYRIGHTS looks like this:

[R O S] SYS:LOGIN
[R O S] SYS:PUBLIC
[RWCO SM] SYS:MAIL/B00001B
[RWCODPSM] SYS:DIANA
[R O S] SYS:MENU
[R O S] SYS:WP51

8. Add explanations.

   You may want to comment on how and why the tree is organized this way. For example,

   A. Give a general explanation of each directory's purpose. (You may want to delete the directories that you don't want to tell the user about—for example most users don't need to know about directories such as SYS:LOGIN, SYS:PUBLIC, and SYS:MAIL.)

THE NETWARE 286 MANUAL MAKER

B. Mention which directories contain applications and utilities, and which contain data files.

C. Point out the user's home directory, if you have created one.

D. Explain which directories contain shared files, such as database files, and tell who else has access to such directories.

You will also want to tell the user what he or she can do in each directory (create files, look at files, organize a structure beneath, etc.). Use the rights sets as your guide as you do this.

The MYRIGHTS file, with explanations, now looks like this:

[R O S]   Diana has these rights in the LOGIN directory, that contains the files needed to log in to the network; the PUBLIC directory contains the NetWare utilities and other system files; the MENU directory contains files needed to run custom menus; and the WP51 directory contains word processing application files. Diana has Read, Open, and Search rights in these directories because she needs to run the programs they contain. She doesn't have any other rights because she shouldn't be able to delete, rename, or otherwise modify these files.

[W C   ]   Diana has the Write and Create rights in the MAIL directory. This creates a "drop-box" directory, where Diana can only create files. The files created in this directory have to do with the NetWare electronic mail system.

[RWOCDPSM]   Diana has all rights in her home directory (DIANA), and the directories beneath it (MYM and WORDPROC). Thus, she has all privileges here.

WORKING WITH DIRECTORIES AND FILES

If you want to actually see your effective rights in any of these directories, complete these steps.

1. Access FILER.

2. Go to the directory by choosing "Select Current Directory."

3. Choose "Current Directory Information."

4. Choose "Current Effective Rights."

Your effective rights are shown in a display similar to the following:

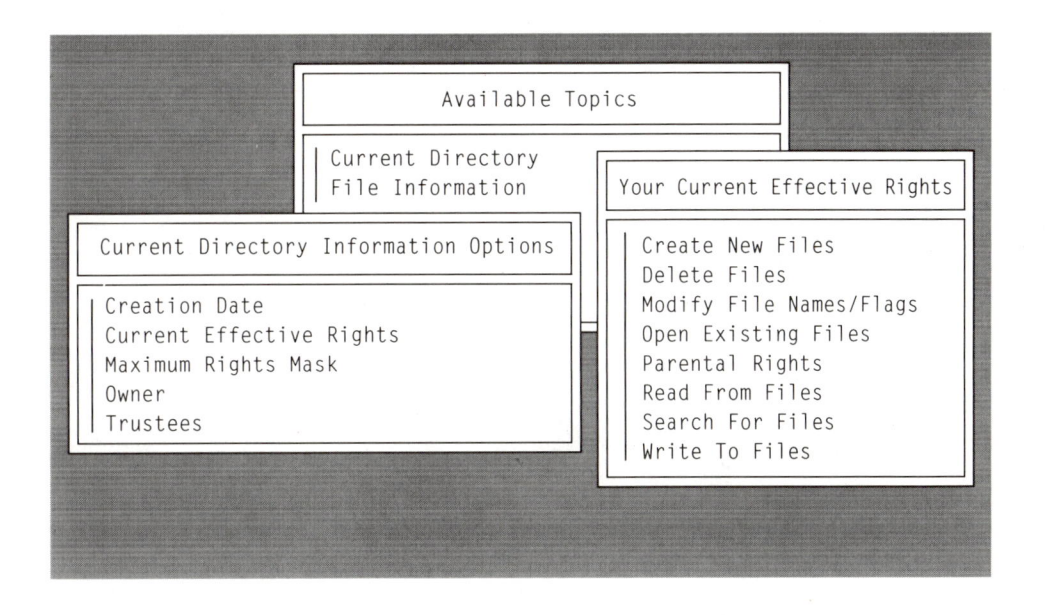

```
                    Available Topics
              ┌─────────────────────────┐
              │ Current Directory       │
              │ File Information        │  Your Current Effective Rights
              │                         ┌──────────────────────────────┐
   Current Directory Information Options│ Create New Files             │
  ┌──────────────────────────────┐      │ Delete Files                 │
  │ Creation Date                │      │ Modify File Names/Flags      │
  │ Current Effective Rights     │      │ Open Existing Files          │
  │ Maximum Rights Mask          │      │ Parental Rights              │
  │ Owner                        │      │ Read From Files              │
  │ Trustees                     │      │ Search For Files             │
  └──────────────────────────────┘      │ Write To Files               │
                                        └──────────────────────────────┘
```

NETWORK USER'S GUIDE   159

THE NETWARE 286 MANUAL MAKER

Network Security, Approach #3: Advanced

This approach offers a complete explanation of security, including effective rights, trustee rights, maximum rights masks, and attributes. I recommend it for advanced users when

- You have given them the Parental right in some directories and expect them to assign security in those directories

- You want to train those users to be as independent as possible

- You expect them to troubleshoot

Refer to the example of customized security on page 156 .

WORKING WITH DIRECTORIES AND FILES

How Your Effective Rights Were Determined

Your effective rights, the rights you can actually exercise in a directory, are determined by the following:

- The security privileges granted to you as a user ("**trustee rights**").

- The security privileges that a directory allows ("**maximum rights mask**").

To have an effective right in a given directory, your trustee rights for the directory must include the right, and so must the directory's rights mask. If you want to see how your effective rights for a directory were determined, you need to see both your trustee rights for the directory and the directory's maximum rights mask. Here is how to do so.

To see a directory's maximum rights mask,

1. Access FILER.

2. Choose "Current Directory Information."

To see the directory's trustees and their rights, continue with these steps.

3. Choose the "(see list)" field next to the "Trustees" label at the bottom of the screen.

If you are a trustee of the directory, you are listed, along with your trustee rights for the directory.

THE NETWARE 286 MANUAL MAKER

Security Attributes

In addition to your effective rights, security attributes may affect what you can do with the files in a particular directory.

Security attributes apply to all users, regardless of their effective rights. They are used mainly as a safeguard against mistakes on the part of any user. Here a description of what they are and what they affect.

Read Write/Read Only—Files in directories marked Read Write can be read from and written to; files in directories marked Read Only cannot be changed, only read.

Shareable/Non-Shareable—Files in directories marked Shareable can be opened by more than one user at a time; files in directories marked Non-Shareable can only be opened by one user at a time.

To see the security attributes of a directory's files, complete these steps:
1. Access FILER; 2. Choose "File Information;" 3. Choose the file; 4. Choose "Attributes."

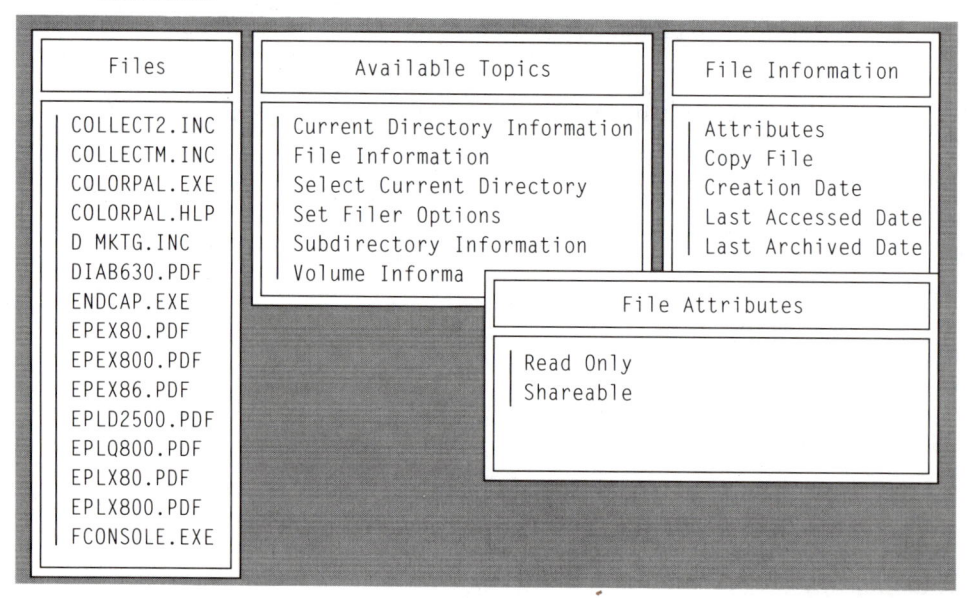

```
┌─────────────────┐ ┌──────────────────────────────┐ ┌──────────────────────┐
│      Files      │ │       Available Topics       │ │   File Information   │
├─────────────────┤ ├──────────────────────────────┤ ├──────────────────────┤
│ COLLECT2.INC    │ │ Current Directory Information│ │ Attributes           │
│ COLLECTM.INC    │ │ File Information             │ │ Copy File            │
│ COLORPAL.EXE    │ │ Select Current Directory     │ │ Creation Date        │
│ COLORPAL.HLP    │ │ Set Filer Options            │ │ Last Accessed Date   │
│ D MKTG.INC      │ │ Subdirectory Information     │ │ Last Archived Date   │
│ DIAB630.PDF     │ │ Volume Informa               └─┴──────────────────────┘
│ ENDCAP.EXE      │ │                  ┌──────────────────────┐
│ EPEX80.PDF      │ │                  │    File Attributes   │
│ EPEX800.PDF     │ │                  ├──────────────────────┤
│ EPEX86.PDF      └─┘                  │ Read Only            │
│ EPLD2500.PDF                         │ Shareable            │
│ EPLQ800.PDF                          └──────────────────────┘
│ EPLX80.PDF      
│ EPLX800.PDF     
│ FCONSOLE.EXE    
└─────────────────┘
```

WORKING WITH DIRECTORIES AND FILES

Looking at Files

> Vital for most users.

To see a directory's files,

1. Access FILER.

2. Choose "File Information."

3. The directory's files are listed in a display similar to the following.

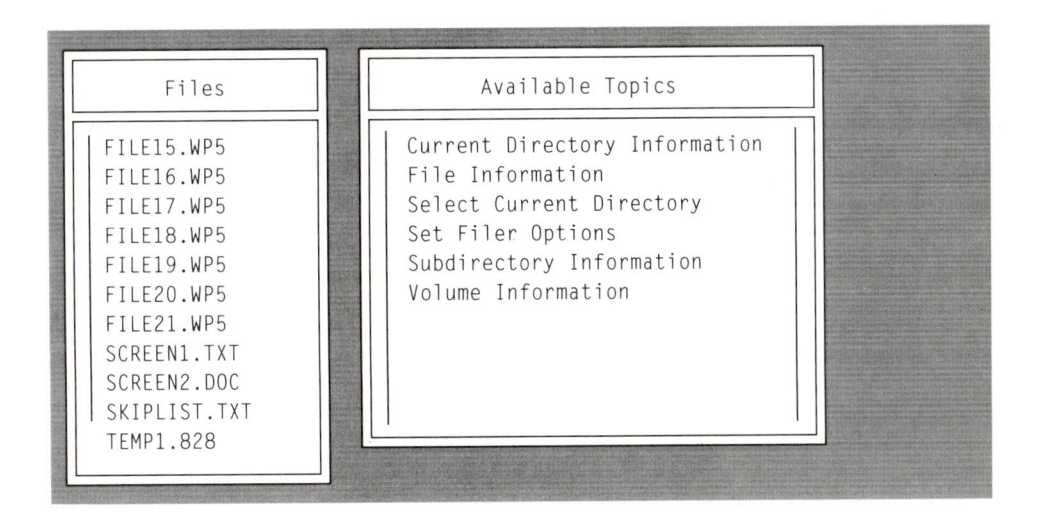

```
┌─────────────────────┐  ┌──────────────────────────────┐
│        Files        │  │       Available Topics       │
├─────────────────────┤  ├──────────────────────────────┤
│ FILE15.WP5          │  │ Current Directory Information│
│ FILE16.WP5          │  │ File Information             │
│ FILE17.WP5          │  │ Select Current Directory     │
│ FILE18.WP5          │  │ Set Filer Options            │
│ FILE19.WP5          │  │ Subdirectory Information     │
│ FILE20.WP5          │  │ Volume Information           │
│ FILE21.WP5          │  │                              │
│ SCREEN1.TXT         │  │                              │
│ SCREEN2.DOC         │  │                              │
│ SKIPLIST.TXT        │  │                              │
│ TEMP1.828           │  │                              │
└─────────────────────┘  └──────────────────────────────┘
```

NETWORK USER'S GUIDE

THE NETWARE 286 MANUAL MAKER

Copying Files

To copy files, complete these steps.

1. Access FILER.

2. Go to the directory you want to copy your files from (the "source" directory).

    NOTE: If you are copying your files from floppy diskettes or a local hard drive, you will have to use COPY or NCOPY. FILER cannot copy FROM a local drive, although it can copy TO a local drive.

3. Choose "File Information."

4. Choose the file(s) you want to copy. To choose more than one, use F5 to mark each.

5. Choose "Copy File" (if you want to leave a copy of the file at the source) or "Move File" (if you don't want a copy left at the source).

6. Specify the destination (target) directory. If you know it, just type it in. If you don't, press INSERT and choose directories until you've specified it. Then press ESCAPE and ENTER.

7. Specify the file's name. If you want it to have the same name, accept the default. If you want to rename it, type a new name. Then press ENTER.

WORKING WITH DIRECTORIES AND FILES

Deleting and Renaming Files

From time to time, you need to "clean up" and reorganize your files. That is when you will want to know how to delete and rename them. Here is how.

1. Access FILER.

2. Go to the directory which contains the files you want to delete or rename.

3. Choose "File Information."

4. To DELETE files,

Highlight the file you want to delete. (To choose more than one, use F5 to mark each.)

Press DELETE.

Answer "Yes" when you're asked if you want to delete the file(s).

5. To RENAME a file,

Highlight the file.

Press MODIFY (F3).

Type the file's new name.

Press ENTER.

NETWORK USER'S GUIDE   165

THE NETWARE 286 MANUAL MAKER

Backing Up and Restoring Files

> You may want to substitute a short explanation of your backup policy for the generic paragraph below. If you have diskless workstations or don't require users to back up their files, delete this section.

Even though we back up network files regularly, you should still back up your personal files as a precaution. You don't need to back up all your files every day; just back up the ones you have modified that day.

For most users, the simplest thing to do is to back up to a floppy diskette, as explained here.

To back up your files, just copy them to a floppy diskette by completing these steps.

1. Access FILER.

2. Go to the directory which contains the files you want to copy.

3. Choose "File Information."

4. Highlight the file you want to copy.

5. Press ENTER.

6. Choose "Copy File."

7. Specify the drive for the floppy diskette you want to copy the file(s) to (A: or B:).

8. Press ENTER, and the file(s) are copied.

WORKING WITH DIRECTORIES AND FILES

Printing Files

> If you use a third-party printing program on your network, you will want to substitute instructions for using that printing program for the NetWare printing instructions given here.

> Generally, I don't recommend that you teach users the details of how NetWare printing works, or how to print their files with the NetWare command line interface. This is why.
>
> - For most users, it is much easier to print using applications. If you set up network printing properly and test it thoroughly, printing from applications should be transparent to users.
>
> - NetWare printing is complex, and users need to understand it fairly well to be comfortable with the NetWare printing utilities. Generally, it makes more sense to set up custom menus for users to print from than to educate users about the many printing parameters.
>
> - If users need to print with CAPTURE, it makes more sense to include the CAPTURE TI=n command in their login scripts or a batch file than to try to teach them how CAPTURE works (see the explanation of CAPTURE in Chapter 6, "Command Line Utilities Reference").

> However, if you do want to teach your users how to print from the command line, you can include this short explanation of NetWare printing and the NPRINT command in their manuals.

Printing on a network is a little more involved than printing with a regular personal computer. Instead of going directly from your personal computer to the printer, print data must follow a somewhat more complex path. This path was set up when the network was installed, so you shouldn't have to worry about it. But briefly, it is as follows.

NETWORK USER'S GUIDE

THE NETWARE 286 MANUAL MAKER

First, the print data ("print job" in NetWare terms) goes to a network print queue, located on the file server's hard disk. Like the personal computer's buffer or spool area, the print queue is a waiting area for print jobs that pile up faster than they can be printed. However, a network print queue can have multiple print queues and each can store jobs from many different users. Which queue your print jobs go to depends on how network printing has been set up, or which queue you specify when you print the job.

> You may want to tell them which print queue(s) their print jobs will go to, and why, here.

A process within the NetWare operating system, called a print server, takes print jobs out of the queue and sends them to the printer. As with print queues, print servers are established when network printing is set up. Which queues a print server services, and which printers it sends print jobs to, depends on how network printing was set up.

> You may want to tell them which printer(s) their print jobs will go to, and why, here.

Luckily, you don't really need to know all this information to print a file. If the file was created in a network application or text editor, just print it from there. If the file was created in a non-network application or text editor, you can print it with NPRINT. The following section summarizes how this is done.

Type ...	To ...
NPRINT *filename*	Print a file created in a non-network application or text editor
NPRINT *filename* NOTIFY	Be notified when the job has printed
NPRINT *filename* C=*n*	Print a certain number of copies (replace *n* with the desired number)

WORKING WITH DIRECTORIES AND FILES

Working with Directories

Most of the time, when you clean up and reorganize, you are working with files. But sometimes you need to work with the directory structure itself.

The following section summarizes how to create, rename, and delete directories, as well as how to copy directory structures.

Create a Subdirectory

1. Access FILER.

2. Move to the directory where you would like to create the subdirectory, if you're not already there.

3. Choose "Subdirectory Information."

4. Press INSERT.

5. Type the new directory's name and press ENTER.

THE NETWARE 286 MANUAL MAKER

Rename a Directory

1. Access FILER.

2. Move to the subdirectory's parent directory.

3. Choose "Subdirectory Information."

4. Highlight the directory you want to rename.

5. Press MODIFY (F3).

6. Type the directory's new name.

7. Press ENTER.

Delete a Directory

1. Access FILER.

2. Move to the subdirectory's parent directory.

3. Choose "Subdirectory Information."

4. Highlight the directory you want to delete.

5. Press DELETE.

6. Answer "Yes" when asked if you want to delete the directory.

WORKING WITH DIRECTORIES AND FILES

Ideas for Creating Your Own Directory Structure

The directory structure for the file server organizes files for everyone who works on the file server. In the areas where you keep your own personal files, you may want to create your own limited directory structures to organize your files. In fact, if you have more than a few files, this is a good idea; you shouldn't dump your electronic files onto a computer without organizing them any more than you would dump your paper files onto a desk or into a drawer.

As you plan your directory structure, consider these questions.

1. What will I organize my files based on?

   Consider what files you have to manage, and what kind of a structure would help you best organize them. It may be useful to think of how you would organize ordinary paper files efficiently, and use that as a guideline for planning your directory structure.

2. Will other people need to access my files?

   If so, it may make sense to put files that need to be accessed by the same people in the same directories.

3. What should I name my directories?

   Give your directories meaningful, descriptive names.

4. How many levels deep should I make my directory structure?

   Generally, it is best not to make the directory structure more than 3-4 levels deep.

THE NETWARE 286 MANUAL MAKER

If you start getting a lot of files in a directory, consider subdividing the directory and reorganizing your files.

Once you have decided how you want to organize your personal directory structures, use the DOS MD command to create directories according to your plan.

Move to the directory which you would like to create the subdirectory beneath. Then type

    MD directory

Substitute the name of your new directory for *directory*. Remember, it can only be eight characters long; if you type a longer name, it is truncated to eight characters.

WORKING WITH DIRECTORIES AND FILES

Setting Up Drive Mappings

> Most users probably won't need to set up drive mappings, and even fewer need to set up search drive mappings. The main reason to set up a search drive mapping is if the user uses personal applications on the network.
>
> In addition, drive and search drive mappings consume directory entries. If you are concerned excessive drive mappings consuming directory entries, you may not want to teach your users how to set up mappings.
>
> Also, if you didn't include the previous sections explaining drive and search drive mappings, you won't want to include this section either.

You probably won't need to set up drive mappings to your newly-created subdirectories unless your subdirectory structure is quite deep and complex. In most cases, it is easier to use your existing drive mappings to get to the general area, then move up and down the directory structure. But if you do want to set up drive mappings, here is how to do it.

1. Access SESSION.

2. Choose "Drive Mappings."

3. Press INSERT.

4. Press ENTER.

5. Choose subdirectories until you have specified the directory you want to map the drive to.

6. Press ESCAPE.

7. Press ENTER.

NETWORK USER'S GUIDE 173

THE NETWARE 286 MANUAL MAKER

Saving Mappings in Login Scripts

> This section tells how to save mappings in personal login scripts. Include it only if you want to teach users about their login scripts. Also, if you teach users how to save drive mappings in their login scripts, caution them not to inadvertently override the mappings contained in the system-wide login script.

Drive mappings set up at the command line last only until you log out. Most of the time, you want your drive mappings to be more permanent than that. To have your drive mappings set up every time you log in, you must save them in your login script.

To do so, complete the following steps:

1. Access the SYSCON utility.

2. Choose "User Information."

3. Choose your name.

4. Choose Login Script.

    You will see your login script. It may have many or few commands, depending on how your supervisor has set it up. Be very careful when you are working in the login script. Make sure you understand the intent of each line before you make any changes.

5. To set the drive mapping, type

MAP *n:=directory path

6. Exit SYSCON, saving your changes.

Now log in again. Type MAP to display your drive mappings (if they aren't shown when you log in). You should see the drive mapping(s) you added.

WORKING WITH DIRECTORIES AND FILES

Setting Security

> Setting security is a fairly advanced topic that most users won't really be concerned with. If you have set up the high-level directory structure properly, users shouldn't have to worry about other users accessing their personal files. Some users may create files in their personal directories that they share with other users; these are probably the only users who might be concerned with setting security.
>
> Remember, unless you have given a user the Parental right in a directory, he or she cannot set security anyway. So you will want to skip this section in manuals you create for users who don't have Parental rights anywhere.
>
> Also, if you include this section, make sure you included the full explanation of security previously, since users need to understand maximum rights masks and trustee rights before they set security.

In the directories where you have the Parental right, you can set security if you want. Unless you will create directories or files that you need to share with other users, you probably won't need to do this, however.

If you do need to assign security, follow these steps.

1. Decide which users need which rights in your directories.

    You may want to sketch the directory tree and write in the names of users who need access to certain directories, along with what rights they should be given. Remember, once you have granted a trustee right in a directory, the right trickles down the tree. So you may not need to actually make trustee assignments in every single directory where you want the user to have security privileges.

NETWORK USER'S GUIDE 175

THE NETWARE 286 MANUAL MAKER

2. Decide if you want to limit the rights that can be exercised in any given directory.

    Sometimes, you will want to be sure that a certain right cannot be exercised in a given directory. For example, you may want to make sure that no one can delete files in a given directory. When this is the case, set the directory's rights mask so the directory doesn't allow the right to be exercised. For example, if you didn't want anyone to be able to delete files in a directory, you would remove the Delete right from the directory's rights mask. Remember, if you remove a right from the maximum rights mask, you remove it for all trustees except the Supervisor (including yourself).

    If you sketched out the directory tree, you may want to write in the directory rights masks on your sketch.

3. Check to be sure that the trustee assignments and directory rights masks that you have planned gives users the rights you want them to have in your directories.

4. Make trustee assignments.

    For each directory where you want to make a trustee assignment,

    1. Access FILER.

    2. Go to the parent directory of the directory where you want to make the trustee assignment(s).

    3. Choose "Subdirectory Information."

    4. Choose the subdirectory where you want to grant the rights.

WORKING WITH DIRECTORIES AND FILES

5. Choose "Trustees" and the directory's current trustees are shown. Most likely, there won't be any yet.

6. Press INSERT.

7. Choose the user(s) and/or group(s) you want to make trustees of the directory.

Now that the trustees are added, change their rights if necessary.

1. Choose the trustee(s) whose rights you want to change. To choose more than one, mark each with F5.

2. The current trustee rights are shown. To remove a right, highlight it and press DELETE. To remove more than one, mark each right you want to remove, press F5 and then press DELETE.

3. Choose "Yes."

Complete the previous three steps for every trustee assignment you want to make. Remember that trustee rights filter down through the directory structure, so you needn't make a trustee assignment in every subsequent directory where you want a user to have rights.

NETWORK USER'S GUIDE   **177**

THE NETWARE 286 MANUAL MAKER

4. Change directory maximum rights masks, if necessary, by completing these steps.

    1. Access FILER.

    2. Choose "Subdirectory Information."

    3. Choose the bracketed field next to "Inherited Rights Mask" at the bottom of the screen.

    4. To delete a right from the mask,

        a. Highlight the right(s).

        b. Press DELETE.

        c. Answer "Yes."

WORKING WITH DIRECTORIES AND FILES

Conclusion

> The following generic conclusion is based on the unmodified Manual Maker text for this chapter. Modify it based on how you modified the chapter.

In this chapter, you learned about

- Directory structures, directory paths, and directory names

- Moving around the directory structure with FILER and drive mappings

- NetWare security and how it controls what you can do on the network

- Working with files, including listing, copying, deleting, renaming, backing up and restoring, printing, and purging

- Working with directories, including listing, creating, copying, deleting, and renaming

- Setting up your own drive mappings

- Establishing security in your personal areas of the directory structure

NETWORK USER'S GUIDE

CHAPTER OVERVIEW

Command Line Utilities Reference

The text for this boilerplate chapter is found in
CLUS.WP (WordPerfect version)
CLUS.ASC (ASCII version)

This chapter features simple explanations of the NetWare command line utilities. Only utilities of use to non-administrative users are included.

For the sake of simplicity, these explanations don't include every available task and option; rather, the most common tasks and options are included. But remember, you can always add to or delete from the explanations given here, based on your needs.

COMMAND LINE UTILITIES REFERENCE

Deciding What Utilities to Include

You can include whatever utilities you want in your user manuals, of course. (You can even add non-NetWare utilities used on your network if you like.) But if you don't know exactly which utilities you want to include, the following comments may help you decide. You can also use the comments contained throughout the Manual Maker.

Delete these utilities if ...	Utility	Page
... the user never needs to work with more than one file server.	ATTACH	189
	SLIST	236
	WHOAMI	242
... the user doesn't know anything at all about security.	FLAG	199
	FLAGDIR	202
	GRANT	204
	REMOVE	226
If the user does know about security, include utilities based on the user's knowledge:	REVOKE	229
	RIGHTS	232
	TLIST	238
Delete these utilities if the user never assigns security.	GRANT	204
	REMOVE	226
	REVOKE	229
	TLIST	238
Delete utilities if the user doesn't know about security attributes.	FLAG	199
	FLAGDIR	202
If the user knows anything about security at all, you should probably INCLUDE this utility.	RIGHTS	232

NETWORK USER'S GUIDE

THE NETWARE 286 MANUAL MAKER

Delete these utilities if ...	Utility	Page
... the user always uses an AUTOEXEC.BAT file to log in.	LOGIN	209
... the user never needs to check the system time	SYSTIME	237
... the user never needs to see space usage information.	CHKVOL	195
... users won't use the NetWare SEND command to send messages.	CASTOFF/ CASTON SEND USERLIST	192 234 241
... the user doesn't know anything about network printing.	CAPTURE	190
... the user doesn't know about drive mappings.	MAP	211
... the user doesn't know about directory structures	CD LISTDIR NDIR	194 207 218

COMMAND LINE UTILITIES REFERENCE

Delete these utilities if ...	Utility	Page
... the user never modifies any area of the directory structure	MD RD RENDIR	215 225 228
... users never change their passwords of their own accord (because you require forced password changes)	SETPASS	235
... the user never deletes or renames files	DEL REN	196 227
the user never copies files	NCOPY	216

THE NETWARE 286 MANUAL MAKER

Making a Master List of Users' Rights

In many cases, a user must have certain rights in order to perform a task. These cases are noted throughout this chapter. Sample text is also provided if you want to tell users what directories they can do certain tasks in.

Before you begin modifying this chapter, you may want to print a master list of users' rights throughout the directory tree. Here are the steps.

1. Log in as the user.

(Note: If passwords are used on your network, you'll have to assign users new passwords or ask them to tell you their passwords. If you don't want to do this, you may wish to have users complete steps 2 and 3, then give you the resulting list.)

2. List the user's effective rights throughout the tree by typing

WHOAMI /R

3. Print the resulting list by completing these steps.

A. Type

CAPTURE TI=10

B. Press the SHIFT and PRTSCR keys simultaneously.

Keep this printed list handy as you work through this chapter.

CHAPTER 6

Command Line Utilities Reference

This chapter explains the Command Line utilities in reference form. The utilities covered are listed below in alphabetical order.

> Note to WordPerfect users: The following list was created with the WordPerfect Cross-Reference feature. When you are finished creating your manual, regenerate this list (see Chapter 8, "Instructions for Final Formatting").

Page	Utility
189	ATTACH
190	CAPTURE
192	CASTOFF/CASTON
194	CD
195	CHKVOL
196	DEL
197	DIR
199	FLAG
202	FLAGDIR
204	GRANT
207	LISTDIR
209	LOGIN
210	LOGOUT

THE NETWARE 286 MANUAL MAKER

Page	Utility
211	MAP
215	MD
216	NCOPY
218	NDIR
223	NPRINT
225	RD
226	REMOVE
227	REN
228	RENDIR
229	REVOKE
232	RIGHTS
234	SEND
235	SETPASS
236	SLIST
237	SYSTIME
238	TLIST
241	USERLIST
242	WHOAMI

COMMAND LINE UTILITIES REFERENCE

Attach

> Include if
>
> - Network has more than one file server
>
> - User has an account on more than one of those servers
>
> - User accesses those accounts manually (not via a batch file or login script)

> If the user accesses an additional server more often than not, you may want to include the appropriate ATTACH command in his or her login script. This way, the user attaches to the additional server automatically upon logging in. All the user has to do is enter a password, if one is required.

Access additional servers once you've logged in to your primary server.

Task	Type
Attach to another file server	ATTACH *fileserver/username*
	Then enter password if prompted.
	Example:
	ATTACH GADFLY/STEVE

NETWORK USER'S GUIDE

THE NETWARE 286 MANUAL MAKER

Capture

> Include if user
>
> - Prints documents not created in network applications
>
> - Does such printing manually (not via menus, login scripts, or batch files)

> Unless you have advanced, inquisitive users who often print outside applications, I recommend that you don't teach users about CAPTURE. Instead, include this command in their login scripts or the system login script:
>
> CAPTURE TI=10
>
> This way, the local LPT port is captured when users log in, and they can print as usual, by pressing SHIFT + PRT SCR. Print jobs are automatically sent to the printer after 10 seconds (or the time you specify after the TImeout parameter—you may want to use a larger number if print jobs use soft fonts or high level graphics).

COMMAND LINE UTILITIES REFERENCE

Print files not created in a network application. The Create option also allows you to save print output to a network file.

Task	Type
Print from non-network application without exiting from it	CAPTURE TI=10
Print upon entering or exiting an application	CAPTURE AUTOENDCAP
Store print output in a file	CAPTURE CR=*filename*
Be told when your job has printed	CAPTURE TI=10 NOTIfy
Print more than one copy of a job	CAPTURE TI=10 C=*number*

NETWORK USER'S GUIDE 191

THE NETWARE 286 MANUAL MAKER

CASTOFF/CASTON

Include if users

- Send messages with SEND or SESSION

- Want to block such messages from time to time (if many messages are sent across the network, and they don't want to be interrupted)

CASTOFF/CASTON were originally developed because when a message sent with SEND (or SESSION) is received, the message stops workstation processing until it is cleared by pressing CTRL-ENTER. If a user is away from a station when a message is received, any processing being done at the station is disabled until the user returns and clears the message. CASTOFF solves this potential problem by allowing a user disable to message reception at the workstation; CASTON then allows the user to re-enable message reception.

CASTOFF is also useful when a user wants to avoid interruptions.

Teach your users about CASTOFF/CASTON if you want. Or, you can analyze when users might need to use CASTOFF (What tasks do they perform that involve lengthy processing that shouldn't be interrupted?). Then, set up a batch file to begin the task, and include CASTOFF in the batch file.

If a user is certain that he or she doesn't want to be interrupted by network messages, include CASTOFF in his or her login script. Or, you can create a group (for example, "Hermits"), and include all such users in the group. Then, in the system login script, include this line:

IF MEMBER_OF_GROUP "HERMITS" THEN #CASTOFF

COMMAND LINE UTILITIES REFERENCE

Block messages sent from all network stations; enable your workstation to receive messages again.

Task	Type
Block messages sent to you with SEND or SESSION	CASTOFF
Enable your workstation to receive messages again	CASTON

THE NETWARE 286 MANUAL MAKER

CD (DOS Change Directory Command)

> Include if user
>
> - Knows about directory structures (all users except extreme novices should)
>
> - Moves up and down in the directory structure manually (not with drive mappings or menus)

Move up and down the directory structure.

Task	Type
Move up one directory level	CD ..
Move up two directory levels	CD ...
Move to the root directory	CD \
Move down one directory level	CD *subdirectory*
	Example:
	CD PERSONAL
Move down two directory levels	CD *subdir\subdir*
	Example:
	CD PERSONAL\LETTERS

COMMAND LINE UTILITIES REFERENCE

CHKVOL

> Include if user
>
> - Is concerned with managing space on file server
>
> - Does troubleshooting that involves checking space usage information (such as checking to see why a file cannot be saved)

See information about the space on a volume.

CHKVOL can only be used on network drives. If you try to check a local drive, there is no response. Also, if you try to check a non-existent drive, there is no response.

Task	Type
See space usage statistics for a volume	CHKVOL *volume*
See space usage statistics for all volumes on server	CHKVOL *

THE NETWARE 286 MANUAL MAKER

DEL (DOS Delete Command)

> Include if user
>
> - Deletes files (requires Delete right)
>
> - Deletes file with operating system (not just in applications)

> Erase a file.
>
> Since users cannot delete files unless they have the Delete right in a directory, you may wish to list the directories where the user has this right. You can use the following sample text to do so if you wish.

On our network, you can delete files in the following directories:

<List the directories where the user has the DELETE right here; refer to your master list of the user's rights throughout the directory tree if desired (see page 186 of the unmodified Manual Maker).>

Task	Type
Erase a file (in your current directory)	DEL *filename*
Erase a file (not in your current directory)	DEL *path filename*

196   NETWORK USER'S GUIDE

COMMAND LINE UTILITIES REFERENCE

DIR (DOS Directory Command)

> Include if user
>
> - Lists files and directories (all users except extreme novices should; requires Search right)
>
> - Lists files with operating system (not just in applications)

List a directory's files.

> Depending on your users' level of sophistication, you may also wish to include the following note:

You must have the appropriate security privileges to list a directory's files. If you don't, no files are shown, although they may exist.

> Since users cannot list files unless they have the Search right in a directory, you may also wish to list the directories where the user has this right. You can use the following sample text to do so if you wish.

THE NETWARE 286 MANUAL MAKER

On our network, you can list files in the following directories:

<List the directories where the user has the Search right here; refer to your master list of the user's rights throughout the directory tree if desired (see page 186 of the unmodified Manual Maker).>

Task	Type
List a directory's files and subdirectories, along with the dates they were last modified	DIR
List files and subdirectories (wide display)	DIR /W
List files and subdirectories, with a pause when the screen is	DIR MORE

COMMAND LINE UTILITIES REFERENCE

FLAG

> Include if user
>
> - Understands NetWare security attributes
>
> - Needs to see file attributes (usually while troubleshooting to find out why a certain task, such as opening a file, cannot be performed)
>
> - Sets attributes for files (requires Search and Modify rights)
>
> Probably very few users check attributes, and fewer still set them.

View or change file attributes.

> Since users cannot change file attributes unless they have the Modify right in a directory, you may wish to list the directories where the user has this right. You can use the following sample text to do so if you wish.

On our network, you can change the attributes of files in the following directories:

<List the directories where the user has the Modify right here; refer to your master list of the user's rights throughout the directory tree if desired (see page 186 of the unmodified Manual Maker).>

NETWORK USER'S GUIDE   199

THE NETWARE 286 MANUAL MAKER

Task

View attributes
(current directory)

Change attributes
(current directory)

View attributes
(not current directory)

Change attributes
(not current directory)

Type

FLAG *filename*

FLAG *filename attributes*

Example:

FLAG INFOBASE S RW
(flags the file INFOBASE Shareable, ReadWrite)

FLAG path

FLAG *path attributes*

Example:

FLAG G:INFOBASE S RW
(flags INFOBASE Shareable, ReadWrite)

A list of the most common file attributes follows.

COMMAND LINE UTILITIES REFERENCE

File Attributes List

Here are the most common file attributes. Use the bolded letters to abbreviate.

Shareable—file can be opened by more than one user at a time
Non**S**hareable—file can only be opened by one user at a time
Read**O**nly—file can be read, but not changed
Read**W**rite—file can be changed
Normal—flags file Non-Shareable, Read Write

THE NETWARE 286 MANUAL MAKER

FLAGDIR

> Include if user
>
> - Understands NetWare security attributes
>
> - Needs to see directory attributes (usually while troubleshooting to find out why a certain task, such as opening a file, cannot be performed)
>
> - Sets attributes for directories (requires Modify right)
>
> Probably very few users check attributes, and fewer still set them.

View or change directory attributes.

> Since users cannot change directory attributes unless they have the Modify right in a directory, you may wish to list the directories where the user has this right. You can use the following sample text to do so if you wish.

On our network, you can change the attributes of the following directories:

<List the directories where the user has the Modify right here; refer to your master list of the user's rights throughout the directory tree if desired (see page 186 of the unmodified Manual Maker).>

COMMAND LINE UTILITIES REFERENCE

Task	Type
View attributes (current directory)	FLAGDIR
Change attributes (current directory)	FLAGDIR *attributes*
View attributes (not current directory)	FLAGDIR *path*
Change attributes (not current directory)	FLAGDIR *path attributes*

Directory Attributes List

Here are the most common directory attributes. Use the bolded letters to abbreviate.

Normal—cancel Hidden and Private attributes if they have been set
Hidden—hides directory
Private—hide subdirectory list from all users except those with Search right in a directory

THE NETWARE 286 MANUAL MAKER

GRANT

> Include if user
>
> - Understands NetWare security thoroughly (including security rights, effective rights, trustee rights, and maximum rights masks)
>
> - Needs to assign trustees in any directories (probably only in personal directories if at all; Parental right required)
>
> Very few users use this command.

Grant users or groups trustee rights in a file or directory.

> Since users cannot grant trustee rights unless they have the Parental right in a directory, you may wish to list the directories where the user has this right. You can use the following sample text to do so if you wish.

On our network, you can grant trustee rights in the following directories:

<List the directories where the user has the Parental right here; refer to your master list of the user's rights throughout the directory tree if desired (see page 186 of the unmodified Manual Maker).>

COMMAND LINE UTILITIES REFERENCE

Task

Grant rights
(current directory)

Grant rights
(not current directory)

Type

GRANT *rights* TO *user*

Example:
GRANT R O S TO VALERIE
(Grants Read, Open, and Search rights to user VALERIE)

GRANT *rights* FOR *path* TO *user*

Example:

GRANT R O S FOR BUSTED TO VALERIE

THE NETWARE 286 MANUAL MAKER

> A brief explanation of the NetWare security rights is contained in the following table. You may wish to include it here for users' convenience.

Here's a brief explanation of the NetWare security rights. To assign a right, use its abbreviation (R for Read, O for Open, etc.).

Letter	Right	Allows you to
R	Read	See the contents of files and execute application files
W	Write	Change the contents of existing files
O	Open	Open files for use
C	Create	Create files and directories
D	Delete	Delete files and directories
P	Parental	Assign security
S	Search	List files in a directory
M	Modify	Change the security attributes of files and directories

COMMAND LINE UTILITIES REFERENCE

LISTDIR

> Include if user
>
> - Knows about directory structures (all users except extreme novices should)
>
> - Lists a directory's subdirectories (Search right required)
>
> Include the /R option if user
>
> - Understands NetWare security thoroughly (most users would look at the mask when troubleshooting to figure out how effective rights were determined. Only users with a thorough understanding of NetWare security—including security rights, effective rights, trustee rights, and maximum rights masks—would ever do this.)

View a directory's subdirectories and their maximum rights masks.

THE NETWARE 286 MANUAL MAKER

Task	Type
View a directory's subdirectories.	LISTDIR
View a directory's subdirectory tree.	LISTDIR /S
View a directory's subdirectories and the maximum rights mask for each.	LISTDIR /R
View a directory's subdirectory tree the maximum rights mask for each directory in it.	LISTDIR /R /S

COMMAND LINE UTILITIES REFERENCE

LOGIN

> Include for all users unless you are certain they will always log in automatically via AUTOEXEC.BAT files.

Log in to a file server.

Task   **Type**

Log in to a file server   LOGIN fileserver/username

                                  Then enter password if prompted.

                                  Example:

                                  LOGIN GADFLY/STEVE

THE NETWARE 286 MANUAL MAKER

LOGOUT

> Include for all users.

Log out from a file server.

You should always log out when you are finished working on the network, or if you are going to be away from your workstation for awhile, so unauthorized users cannot use your account.

Task   **Type**

Logout from a file server   LOGOUT

COMMAND LINE UTILITIES REFERENCE

MAP

> Include if user
>
> - Understands directory structures
>
> - Understands mappings

> This explanation of MAP is divided into three sections, that progress from basic to advanced.
>
> - Approach #1 is for users who understand drive mappings and use them, but do not set up drive mappings.
>
> - Approach #2 is for users who understand drive mappings and do set them up.
>
> - Approach #3 is for users who understand search drive mappings.
>
> Each section is self-contained; choose the one you want, and exclude the others.

THE NETWARE 286 MANUAL MAKER

> MAP Approach #1:
>
> For users who
>
> - Understand and use drive mappings, but
>
> - Won't set up their own mappings

View your drive mappings.

Task	Type
View your drive mappings	MAP

COMMAND LINE UTILITIES REFERENCE

> MAP Approach #2:
>
> For users who
>
> - Understand and use drive mappings
>
> - Set up their own drive mappings

View and set your drive mappings.

Task	Type
View your drive mappings	MAP
Set a drive mapping	MAP *driveletter=path*

THE NETWARE 286 MANUAL MAKER

> MAP Approach #3:
>
> For users who
>
> - Understand drive and search drive mappings
>
> - Set up their own drive and search drive mappings

Task   **Type**

View your drive and search drive
mappings   MAP

Set a drive mapping   MAP *driveletter*:=*path*

Set a search drive mapping   MAP S*number:*=*path*

    Remember, drive and search drive mappings set up at the command line last only until you log out. If you want these mappings to be executed every time you log in, include the above commands in your login script (taking care not to override other drive and search drive mappings).

COMMAND LINE UTILITIES REFERENCE

MD (DOS Make Directory Command)

> Include if user
>
> - Understands directory structures
>
> - Creates directory structures (usually under home directory; Parental and Create rights required)

Make a directory.

> Since users cannot create a subdirectory beneath a directory unless they have the Create right in that directory, you may wish to list the directories where the user has this right. You can use the following sample text to do so if you wish.

On our network, you can create directories in the following locations:

<List the directories where the user has the Parental and Create rights here; refer to your master list of the user's rights throughout the directory tree if desired (see page 186 of the unmodified Manual Maker).>

Task   **Type**

Make a directory   MD *directory*

                                  Example:

                                  MD LETTERS

NETWORK USER'S GUIDE   215

THE NETWARE 286 MANUAL MAKER

NCOPY

> Include if user
>
> - Copies files (requires Read, Open, and Search rights in the source directory, and the Write and Create rights in the target directory)
>
> - Copies files with operating system (not just in applications)

Copy files between network directories and/or local drives or hard disks.

> Since users cannot copy files unless they have the appropriate rights, you may wish to list the directories where the user has these rights. You can use the following sample text to do so.

On our network, you can copy files to and from these directories.

Dirs. You Can Copy Files From	**Dirs. You Can Copy Files To**
<List the directories here— User must have Read, Open, and Search rights in them>	<List the directories here— User must have the Write and Create rights in them>

Task	**Type**
Copy file to current directory	NCOPY *path filename*
	Example: NCOPY G:REPORTS
Copy file from current directory to another directory	NCOPY *filename path*
	Example: NCOPY REPORT G:

216   NETWORK USER'S GUIDE

COMMAND LINE UTILITIES REFERENCE

Copy file and rename at the same time   NCOPY *filename newname*

                                                                 Example: NCOPY REPORTS RESEARCH

Copy multiple related files   Use wildcards

                                                                 Example: NCOPY *.BAT

THE NETWARE 286 MANUAL MAKER

NDIR

Include if user

- Lists directories and files (all users except extreme novices should), and does so with operating system (not just in applications)

- Needs to see more information than DIR provides

- Needs to sort and restrict file listings beyond the abilities DIR provides

NDIR is a powerful command that lets you sort and restrict file and directory listings based on all sorts of criteria. Unfortunately, NDIR can also be very complex. You may prefer to have novice users use DIR, since DIR returns less information.

In addition, unless NDIR is used quite often, it can be difficult to remember the syntax. Because of this, you may wish to create a custom menu whose options that call the appropriate variation of the NDIR command, then have users use that menu.

This explanation of NDIR does NOT explain every NDIR option available; for simplicity's sake, I included only those options I thought might be useful to the average nonadministrative user. You can add to, or delete from, my material if you want to, of course.

COMMAND LINE UTILITIES REFERENCE

List files and subdirectories and see information about them. You can also sort and/or restrict the results of lookups based on the criteria you specify.

> Depending on your users' level of sophistication, you may also wish to include the following note:

You must have the appropriate security privileges to list a directory's files. If you don't, no files are shown, although they may exist.

> Since users cannot list files unless they have the Search right in a directory, you may wish to list the directories where the user has this right. You can use the following sample text to do so if you wish.

THE NETWARE 286 MANUAL MAKER

On our network, you can list files of the following directories:

<List the directories where the user has the Search right; refer to your master list of the user's rights throughout the directory tree if desired (see page of the unmodified Manual Maker).>

Task	Type
List a directory's files and subdirectories, and information about them	NDIR .
Sort lists based on size, smallest to largest	NDIR . SORT SIZE
Sort lists based on last update, earliest to latest	NDIR . SORT UPDATE
Sort lists based on when they were last accessed, earliest to latest	NDIR . SORT ACCESS
See only files updated before a certain date	NDIR . UPDATE BEFore *mm-dd-yy* Example: NDIR . UPDATE AFT 01-25-90 (lists only files created before January 25, 1990)

220   NETWORK USER'S GUIDE

COMMAND LINE UTILITIES REFERENCE

See only files updated after   NDIR . UPDATE AFTer *mm-dd-yy*
a certain date

                                                  Example:

                                                  NDIR . UPDATE AFT 01-25-90
                                                  (lists only files created before January 25, 1990)

See only files accessed before   NDIR . ACCESS BEFore *mm-dd-yy*
a certain date

                                                  Example:

                                                  NDIR . ACCESS BEF 02-15-90 FO
                                                  (lists only files accessed before February 15, 1990)

See only files accessed after   NDIR . ACCESS AFTer *mm-dd-yy*
a certain date

                                                  Example:

                                                  NDIR . ACCESS AFT 02-15-90 FO
                                                  (lists only files accessed after February 15, 1990)

See only files created by a   NDIR . OWNER=*username*
certain person

                                                  Example:

                                                  NDIR . OWNER=CHRIS
                                                  (lists only files created by user Chris)

THE NETWARE 286 MANUAL MAKER

See files only (no subdirectories)   NDIR . FO
                                        (FO = Files Only)

See directories only (no files)   NDIR . DO
                                        (DO = Directories Only)

See subdirectory tree under   NDIR . SUB
directory   (SUB = SUBdirectory)

COMMAND LINE UTILITIES REFERENCE

NPRINT

Include if user

- Prints existing, pre-formatted files from outside of network applications

NPRINT offers many options that allow users to specify exactly how they want a job to be printed. However, unless a user understands NetWare printing very well and uses NPRINT quite often, these options can be difficult to remember and use. For this reason, I think it makes more sense to create a menu that calls the relevant NPRINT commands, and have the user use the menu, than to try and train the user about all the available options.

For this reason, the following task table explains only a few NPRINT options. If you include the Form and Printer options, make sure your users know which forms and printers are available.

THE NETWARE 286 MANUAL MAKER

Print existing, previously-formatted files from outside of an application.

Task

Type

Print an existing, previously-formatted file from outside of an application

NPRINT *filename*

Print more than one copy of the file

NPRINT *filename* C=*number*

Print the job on a certain form

NPRINT *filename* FORM=*formname*

Available forms include:

<list and describe forms here>

COMMAND LINE UTILITIES REFERENCE

RD (DOS Remove Directory Command)

> Include if user
>
> - Understands directory structures
>
> - Deletes directories (usually under home directory, while reorganizing files; Delete right required)

Erase a directory.

> Since users cannot erase a directory unless they have the Parental and Delete right in its parent directory, you may wish to list the directories where the user has these rights. You can use the following sample text to do so if you wish.

On our network, you can delete subdirectories beneath these directories:

<List the directories where the user has the Parental and Delete rights here>

Task

Erase directory

Steps

1. Go to the directory's parent directory.

2. Type

   RD *directory*

NETWORK USER'S GUIDE   **225**

THE NETWARE 286 MANUAL MAKER

REMOVE

> Include if user
>
> - Understands NetWare security thoroughly (including security rights, effective rights, trustee rights, and maximum rights masks)
>
> - Needs to remove a trustee from directories (probably only in personal directories if at all; Parental right required)
>
> Few users use this command.

Delete a user or group from the trustee list of a directory.

> Since users cannot remove trustees unless they have the Parental right in a directory, you may wish to list the directories where the user has this right. You can use the following sample text to do so if you wish.

On our network, you can remove trustees from the following directories:

<List the directories where the user has the Parental right here; refer to your master list of the user's rights throughout the directory tree if desired (see page 186 of the unmodified Manual Maker).>

Task	Type
Remove user from current directory	REMOVE *user*
Remove user from all of directory's subdirectories	REMOVE *user subdirectory*

226   NETWORK USER'S GUIDE

COMMAND LINE UTILITIES REFERENCE

REN (DOS Rename command)

> Include if user
>
> - Renames files with operating system (not just in applications). (Most users only do this in personal directories, while reorganizing; the Modify right is required.)

Rename a file.

> Since users cannot rename files unless they have the Modify right in a directory, you may wish to list the directories where the user has this right. You can use the following sample text to do so if you wish.

On our network, you can rename files in these directories:

<List the directories where the user has the Modify right here>

Task	Type
Rename file (in current directory)	REN *filename newname*
	Example: REN MYFILE YOURFILE
Rename file (not in current directory)	REN *path filename newname*
	Example: RENF:MYFILE YOURFILE

NETWORK USER'S GUIDE 227

THE NETWARE 286 MANUAL MAKER

RENDIR

> Include if user
>
> • Renames directories (probably only beneath personal directories, while reorganizing; Modify right required)
>
> • Renames directories with operating system (not just in applications)

Rename a directory.

> Since users cannot rename a directory unless they have the Modify right in the directory's parent directory, you may wish to list the directories where the user has this right. You can use the following sample text to do so if you wish.

On our network, you can rename subdirectories of these directories:

<List the directories where the user has the Modify right here>

Task

Rename directory.

Steps

1. Go to parent directory.

2. Type

       RENDIR *directory newname*

COMMAND LINE UTILITIES REFERENCE

REVOKE

> Include if user
>
> - Understands NetWare security thoroughly (including security rights, effective rights, trustee rights, and maximum rights masks)
>
> - Needs to assign trustee rights in any directories (probably only in personal directories if at all; Parental right required)
>
> Few users use this command.

Revoke certain user's trustee rights in a directory.

> Since a user cannot revoke other users' trustee rights unless the user has the Parental right in a directory, you may wish to list the directories where the user has this right. You can use the following sample text to do so if you wish.

On our network, you can revoke rights in the following directories:

<List the directories where the user has the Parental right here; refer to your master list of the user's rights throughout the directory tree if desired (see page 186 of the unmodified Manual Maker).>

NETWORK USER'S GUIDE

THE NETWARE 286 MANUAL MAKER

Task

Revoke some of a user's rights in a directory

Steps

1. Go to the directory

2. Type

REVOKE *rightslist* from *username*

Example:

REVOKE P M FROM JENNIFER
(revokes user Jennifer's Parental and Modify rights in current directory)

COMMAND LINE UTILITIES REFERENCE

> A brief explanation of the NetWare security rights is contained in the following table. You may wish to include it here for users' convenience.

Here's a brief explanation of the NetWare security rights. To revoke a right, use its abbreviation (R for Read, O for Open, etc.).

Letter	Right	Allows you to
R	Read	See the contents of files and execute application files
W	Write	Change the contents of existing files
O	Open	Open files for use
C	Create	Create files and directories
D	Delete	Delete files and directories
P	Parental	Assign security
S	Search	List files in a directory
M	Modify	Change the security attributes of files and directories

NETWORK USER'S GUIDE

THE NETWARE 286 MANUAL MAKER

RIGHTS

> Include if user
>
> - Knows about NetWare security
>
> - Checks effective rights (usually when troubleshooting to find out why a certain task, such as saving a file, cannot be performed. Only users who understand the NetWare security rights would ever do this.)

See your effective rights in a directory.

Task

See your effective rights
(current directory)

See your effective rights
(not current directory)

Type

RIGHTS

RIGHTS *path*

Example:

RIGHTS H:
(shows you your effective rights for the directory which is mapped to drive H:)

COMMAND LINE UTILITIES REFERENCE

A brief explanation of the NetWare security rights is contained in the following table. You may wish to include it here for users' convenience.

Here's a brief explanation of the NetWare security rights.

Letter	Right	Allows you to
R	Read	See the contents of files and execute application files
W	Write	Change the contents of existing files
O	Open	Open files for use
C	Create	Create files and directories
D	Delete	Delete files and directories
P	Parental	Assign security
S	Search	List files in a directory
M	Modify	Change the security attributes of files and directories

THE NETWARE 286 MANUAL MAKER

SEND

> Include if user
>
> • Sends short messages to other users at the command line

Send a short message (maximum of 45 characters, including username) to another network user or group.

Task

Send a message to a network user or group

Type

SEND "*message*" TO *name*

Example:

To send the message "Want to go to lunch?" to user Kelley, you would type

SEND "WANT TO GO TO LUNCH?" TO KELLEY

Send a message to more than one network user or group

SEND "*message*" TO *name, name*

Example:

To send the message to users Kelley and Ev, you would type

SEND "WANT TO GO TO LUNCH?" TO KELLEY, EV

234 NETWORK USER'S GUIDE

COMMAND LINE UTILITIES REFERENCE

SETPASS

> Include unless
>
> - You are one of very few installations that don't require passwords
>
> - You force periodic password changes and are certain that users only change their passwords then

Change your password.

Task	Steps
Change your password	1. Type SETPASS 2. Type your old password. 3. Type your new password. 4. Retype your new password.

NETWORK USER'S GUIDE   235

THE NETWARE 286 MANUAL MAKER

SLIST

> Include if
>
> - Your network has more than one file server
>
> - Users need to list the file servers that are currently active on the network (most users would do this if they have accounts on more than one server, or wish to send a message to a user on another server)

List the other file servers on your network that your file server can currently communicate with.

Task   **Type**

See the servers which your file   SLIST
server can communicate with

COMMAND LINE UTILITIES REFERENCE

SYSTIME

> Include if user
>
> - Needs to see the system time
>
> - Needs to synchronize workstation time with file server time (if user does time-dependent tasks that require precise synchronization between file server and workstation)

> Very few users should need to use this command.
>
> If it is important for workstation time to remain precisely synchronized with the file server time on your network, I recommend that you include SYSTIME in a login script or batch file. That way, the workstation and file server time is synchronized when the user logs in.

See the file server's date and time, and synchronize your workstation's date and time with it.

Task	Type
See your file server's current time	SYSTIME

THE NETWARE 286 MANUAL MAKER

TLIST

> Include if user
>
> - Understands NetWare security thoroughly (including security rights, effective rights, trustee rights, and maximum rights masks)
>
> - Has the Parental right in any directories (necessary to list trustees)
>
> - Needs to list trustees (the main reason to list trustees in day-to-day use is for troubleshooting. Some users might like to see who else has rights in a directory out of curiosity—mainly in their personal directories—but even this is unlikely)
>
> Few users use this command.

List the trustees of a directory and their rights.

> Since users cannot list the trustees of a directory unless they have the Parental right in the directory, you may wish to list the directories where the user has this right. You can use the following sample text to do so if you wish.

On our network, you can list trustees of the following directories:

<List the directories where the user has the Parental right here; refer to your master list of the user's rights throughout the directory tree if desired (see page 186 of the unmodified Manual Maker).>

COMMAND LINE UTILITIES REFERENCE

Task   **Type**

List trustees   TLIST
(current directory)

List trustees   TLIST *path*
(not current directory)

THE NETWARE 286 MANUAL MAKER

> A brief explanation of the NetWare security rights is contained in the following table. You may wish to include it here for users' convenience.

Here's a brief explanation of the NetWare security rights.

Letter	Right	Allows you to
R	Read	See the contents of files and execute application files
W	Write	Change the contents of existing files
O	Open	Open files for use
C	Create	Create files and directories
D	Delete	Delete files and directories
P	Parental	Assign security
S	Search	List files in a directory
M	Modify	Change the security attributes of files and directories

COMMAND LINE UTILITIES REFERENCE

USERLIST

> Include if users
>
> - List other users logged into the file server (for curiosity, or because the send messages with the SEND command)

List the users who are currently logged in to a server.

Task   **Type**

List users currently logged in to server.   USERLIST

THE NETWARE 286 MANUAL MAKER

WHOAMI

> Include if
>
> - There is more than one file server on the network
>
> - Users periodically logs in to several servers at a time
>
> Include /R, /S, and /G options if
>
> - Users understands network security

View information about yourself as a network user.

Task	Type
See your username and login date/time	WHOAMI
See your effective rights	WHOAMI /R
See your security equivalences	WHOAMI /S
See your group membership	WHOAMI /G
See all of the above information	WHOAMI /A

CHAPTER OVERVIEW

Menu Utilities Reference

The text for this boilerplate chapter is found in
MENU.WP (WordPerfect version)
MENU.ASC (ASCII version)

This chapter features simple explanations of the NetWare menu utilities. Only utilities used by non-administrative users are included, and only tasks used by non-administrative users are documented. Tasks are documented by utility, in sequential order, based on how the utility is constructed.

MENU UTILITIES REFERENCE

Deciding What Tasks to Include

You can include whatever utilities you want in your user manuals, of course. (You can even add non-NetWare utilities used on your network if you like.) But if you don't know exactly which utilities you want to include, comments on the following pages may help you decide. You can also use the comments contained throughout the Manual Maker.

1. Delete these tasks if the user never needs to work with more than one file server.

   Change Current Server, 290
   Change Your Current Server, 298

2. Delete these tasks if the user doesn't know anything at all about security.

   View Directory Owner, Creation Date/Time, Effective Rights, 252-253
   Change Maximum Rights, 253
   View/Change Directory Trustees, 260
   List Groups, 299
   See Group's Full Name, 301
   See Members of Group, 302
   See Trustee Assignments (Groups), 304
   See Trustee Assignments (Your Own), 307
   See the Groups You Belong To, 317
   See Security Equivalences, 320
   See Trustee Directory Assignments, 326

3. Delete this task if you have not established accounting on your server, or if the user doesn't know anything about accounting.

   See Your Account Balance, 310

NETWORK USER'S GUIDE 245

THE NETWARE 286 MANUAL MAKER

4. Delete this task if users never set their passwords of their own accord (because you have set up forced password changes).

   Change Your Password, 315

5. Delete this task if the user doesn't know about login scripts.

   Access Your Login Script, 319

6. Delete these tasks if you have not established the related restrictions, or if you prefer to simply tell the user what the restrictions are.

   See Your Account Restrictions, 311
   See Station Restrictions , 322
   See Time Restrictions, 324
   See Volume Restrictions, 276

7. Delete these tasks if the user doesn't know anything about NetWare printing.

   List Print Jobs, 278
   Print a File, 280
   Print Job Parameters, 282

8. Delete these tasks if the user doesn't know about drive or search drive mappings.

   See/Set Drive Mappings, 291
   See/Set Search Drive Mappings, 293
   Select Default Drive, 295

9. Delete these tasks if the user does not use NetWare to send messages.

MENU UTILITIES REFERENCE

Send a Message to a Group, 292
Send a Message to a User, 296

10. Delete this task if the user doesn't know about volumes.

    See Volume Information, 276

11. Most users won't need to know how to do these tasks. Check the Comments to see if you want to include them.

    Set Filer Options, 275
    See Your Full Name, 316

THE NETWARE 286 MANUAL MAKER

Making a Master List of Users' Rights

In many cases, a user must have certain rights to perform a task. These cases are noted throughout this chapter. Sample text is also provided if you want to tell users what directories they can do certain tasks in.

Before you begin modifying this chapter, you may want to print a master list of users' rights throughout the directory tree. Here are the steps.

1. Log in as the user.

2. Clear the screen by typing

    CLS

3. List the user's effective rights throughout the structure by typing

    WHOAMI /R

4. Print the resulting list by completing these steps.

    A. Type

        CAPTURE TI=10

    B. Press the SHIFT and PRTSCR keys simultaneously.

Keep the printed list handy as you work through this chapter.

CHAPTER 7

Menu Utilities Reference

This chapter explains the Menu utilities in reference form. Here are the tasks that are covered.

Deciding What Tasks to Include 245

Making a Master List of Users' Rights 248

View Directory Creation Date/Time 252

View Effective Rights 253

View/Change Maximum Rights Mask 255

View Directory Owner 259

View/Change Directory Trustees 260

List a Directory's Files and Subdirectories 263

Delete a File 265

Rename a File 266

Copy a File 267

See a File's Attributes 269

Create a Directory 272

Delete a Directory 273

NETWORK USER'S GUIDE   249

THE NETWARE 286 MANUAL MAKER

Rename a Directory 274

Set FILER Options 275

See Volume Information 276

List Print Queues 277

List Print Jobs 278

Print a File 280

Print Job Parameters 282

Delete Print Job 284

Change Order of Print Jobs 285

Place a Hold on a Print Job 287

See Print Queue Status 288

Change Your Current Server 290

See/Set Drive Mappings 291

Send a Message to a Group 292

See/Set Search Drive Mappings 293

Select Default Drive 295

MENU UTILITIES REFERENCE

Send a Message to a User 296

Change Your Current Server 298

List Groups 299

See Group's Full Name 301

See Members of Group 302

See Trustee Assignments (Groups) 304

See Trustee Assignments (Your Own) 307

See Your Account Balance 310

See Your Account Restrictions 311

Change Your Password 315

See Your Full Name 316

See the Groups You Belong To 317

Access Your Login Script 319

See Security Equivalences 320

See Station Restrictions 322

See Time Restrictions 324

See Trustee Directory Assignments 326

NETWORK USER'S GUIDE   251

THE NETWARE 286 MANUAL MAKER

View a Directory's Creation Date (FILER)

> Most users won't need to see when a directory was created. (If they need to see a creation date, it's usually for a file.)

Action   **Display**

1. Access FILER.   FILER "Available Topics" menu

2. Choose "Current Directory   "Current Directory Information" menu
   Information."

3. Choose "Creation Date."   See below

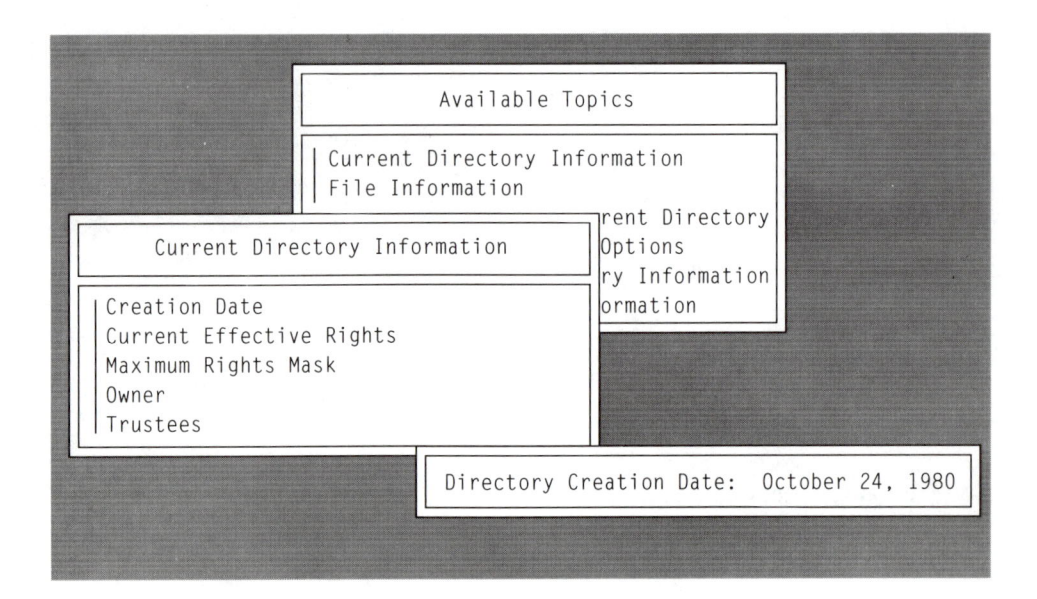

```
         Available Topics
     Current Directory Information
     File Information
                                  rent Directory
     Current Directory Information   Options
                                     ry Information
     Creation Date                   ormation
     Current Effective Rights
     Maximum Rights Mask
     Owner
     Trustees

            Directory Creation Date:  October 24, 1980
```

252   NETWORK USER'S GUIDE

MENU UTILITIES REFERENCE

View Your Effective Rights in a Directory

> Include if user
>
> - Knows about NetWare security
>
> - Checks effective rights (usually when troubleshooting to find out why a certain task, such as saving a file, cannot be performed. Only users who understand the NetWare security rights would ever do this.)

Your effective rights are those you can actually exercise in the directory.

Action	Display
1. Access FILER.	FILER "Available Topics" menu
2. Choose "Current Directory	"Current Directory Information" menu Information."
3. Choose "Current Effective Rights"	See below

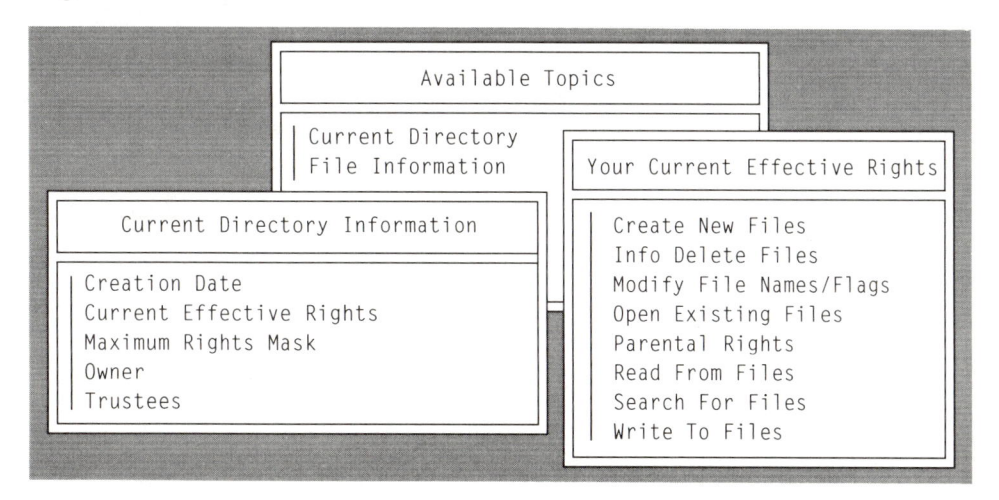

```
                   Available Topics
              Current Directory
              File Information
                              Your Current Effective Rights
      Current Directory Information
                              Create New Files
                              Info Delete Files
  Creation Date               Modify File Names/Flags
  Current Effective Rights    Open Existing Files
  Maximum Rights Mask         Parental Rights
  Owner                       Read From Files
  Trustees                    Search For Files
                              Write To Files
```

NETWORK USER'S GUIDE 253

THE NETWARE 286 MANUAL MAKER

> A brief explanation of the NetWare security rights is contained in the following table. You may want to include it here for users' convenience.

Here is a brief explanation of the Netware security rights.

Letter	Right	Allows you to
R	Read	See the contents of files and execute application files
W	Write	Change the contents of existing files
O	Open	Open files for use
C	Create	Create files and directories
D	Delete	Delete files and directories
P	Parental	Assign security
S	Search	List files in a directory
M	Modify	Change the security attributes of files and directories

MENU UTILITIES REFERENCE

View/Change Maximum Rights Mask (FILER)

> Include if user
>
> - Understands NetWare security thoroughly (including security rights, effective rights, trustee rights, and maximum rights masks
>
> - Needs to see a directory's maximum rights mask (usually when trouble shooting to figure out how effective rights were determined. Only users with a very thorough understanding of NetWare security—including security rights, effective rights, trustee rights, and maximum rights masks—would ever do this)
>
> - Ever assigns security (probably only in personal directories, if at all; Parental right required)

> Since users cannot change the maximum rights mask unless they have the Parental right in a directory, you may want to list the directories where the user has this right. You can use the following sample text to do so if you want.

A directory's maximum rights mask determines which rights can be exercised in the directory.

On our network, you can change the maximum rights mask for the following directories:

<List the directories where the user has the Parental right here; refer to your master list of the user's rights throughout the directory tree if desired (see page 248 of the unmodified Manual Maker).>

THE NETWARE 286 MANUAL MAKER

Action	Display
1. Access FILER.	FILER "Available Topics" menu
2. Choose "Current Directory Information.	"Current Directory Information" menu
3. Choose "Maximum Rights Mask."	"Maximum Rights" menu
4. To add a right to the mask,	
A. Press INSERT.	"Other Rights" list
B. Choose the right(s). (Use F5 to mark more than one.)	"Maximum Rights" menu with rights added
5. To delete a right from the mask,	
A. Highlight the right(s).	
B. Press DELETE.	"Revoke Right" prompt
C. Answer "Yes."	"Maximum Rights" menu with right(s) revoked (see next page)

MENU UTILITIES REFERENCE

Sample "Maximum Rights" menus"

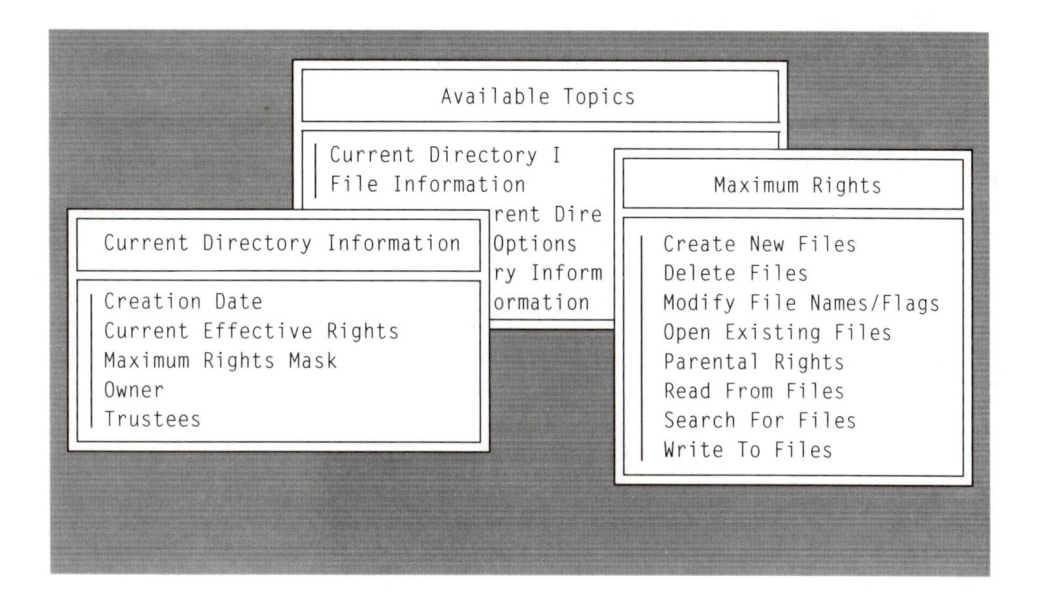

```
┌─────────────────────────────────────────────────────────────┐
│                                                             │
│              ┌──────────────────────────┐                   │
│              │     Available Topics     │                   │
│              ├──────────────────────────┤                   │
│              │ Current Directory I   ┌──────────────────────┤
│              │ File Information      │    Maximum Rights    │
│              │                rent Dir├──────────────────────┤
│   ┌──────────┴────────────────┐Options│ Create New Files     │
│   │ Current Directory Information│ry Inform│ Delete Files    │
│   ├───────────────────────────┤ormation│ Modify File Names/Flags│
│   │ Creation Date             └───────┤ Open Existing Files  │
│   │ Current Effective Rights          │ Parental Rights      │
│   │ Maximum Rights Mask               │ Read From Files      │
│   │ Owner                             │ Search For Files     │
│   │ Trustees                          │ Write To Files       │
│   └───────────────────────────────────┴──────────────────────┘
│                                                             │
└─────────────────────────────────────────────────────────────┘
```

NETWORK USER'S GUIDE

THE NETWARE 286 MANUAL MAKER

> A brief explanation of the NetWare security rights is contained in the following table. You may want to include it here for users' convenience.

Here is a brief explanation of the NetWare security rights.

Letter	Right	Allows you to
R	Read	See the contents of files and execute application files
W	Write	Change the contents of existing files
O	Open	Open files for use
C	Create	Create files and directories
D	Delete	Delete fiels and directories
P	Parental	Assign security
S	Search	List files in a directory.
M	Modify	Change the security attributes of files and directories

MENU UTILITIES REFERENCE

View Directory Owner

> Few users need to see this information.

A directory's owner is the person who created the directory.

Action	**Display**
1. Access FILER.	FILER "Available Topics" menu
2. Choose "Current Directory Information."	"Current Directory Information" menu
3. Choose "Owner."	See below

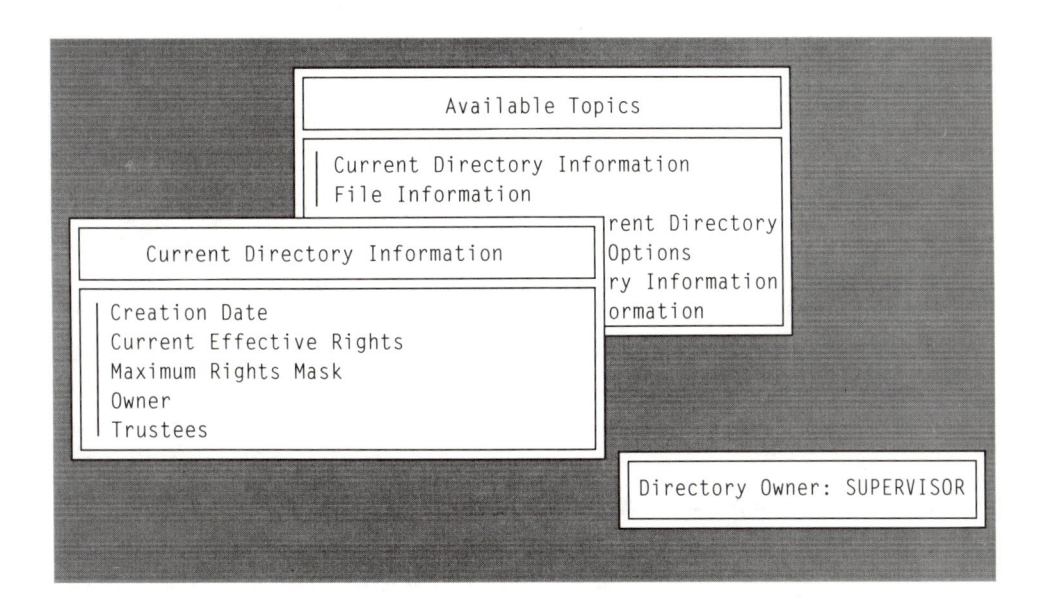

```
                    ┌─────────────────────────────────┐
                    │       Available Topics          │
                    ├─────────────────────────────────┤
                    │ Current Directory Information   │
                    │ File Information                │
         ┌──────────┴──────────────────────┐ rent Directory
         │  Current Directory Information  │ Options
         ├─────────────────────────────────┤ ry Information
         │ Creation Date                   │ ormation
         │ Current Effective Rights        │
         │ Maximum Rights Mask             │
         │ Owner                           │
         │ Trustees                        │
         └─────────────────────────────────┘
                                   ┌──────────────────────────────┐
                                   │ Directory Owner: SUPERVISOR  │
                                   └──────────────────────────────┘
```

THE NETWARE 286 MANUAL MAKER

View/Change Directory Trustees (FILER)

> Include if user
>
> - Understands NetWare security thoroughly (including security rights, effective rights, trustee rights, and maximum rights masks)
>
> - Has the Parental right in any directories (necessary to list or assign trustees)
>
> - Needs to list trustees (the main reason to list trustees in day-to-day use is for troubleshooting. Some users might like to see who else has rights in a directory out of curiosity—mainly in their personal directories—but even this is unlikely)
>
> - Needs to assign trustees in any directories (probably only in personal directories if at all)
>
> Few users use this command.

> Since users cannot view or assign trustees unless they have the Parental right in a directory, you may want to list the directories wher ethe user has this right. You can use the following sample text to do so if you want.

A directory's trustees are those users who have privileges to work with the directory and its files.

On our network, you can chagne the trustees of the following directories:

<List the directories where the user has the Parental right here; refer to your master list of the user's rights throughout the directory tree if desired (see page 248 of the unmodified Manual Maker.>

260   NETWORK USER'S GUIDE

MENU UTILITIES REFERENCE

Action   **Display**

1. Access FILER   FILER "Available Topics" menu

2. Choose "Current Directory   Trustee Name and Type Rights
   Information."

3. Choose "Trustees."   List of trustees and their rights

4. To add a trustee,

   A. Press INSERT.   "Others" list

   B. Choose the user(s) you   List of trustees with new trustees added
      want to make trustees.

5. To delete a trustee,

   A. Highlight trustee(s).

   B. Press DELETE.   "Delete Trustee From Directory" prompt

   C. Choose "Yes."   List of trustees with trustee(s) deleted
                                                    (see screen next page)

NETWORK USER'S GUIDE   261

THE NETWARE 286 MANUAL MAKER

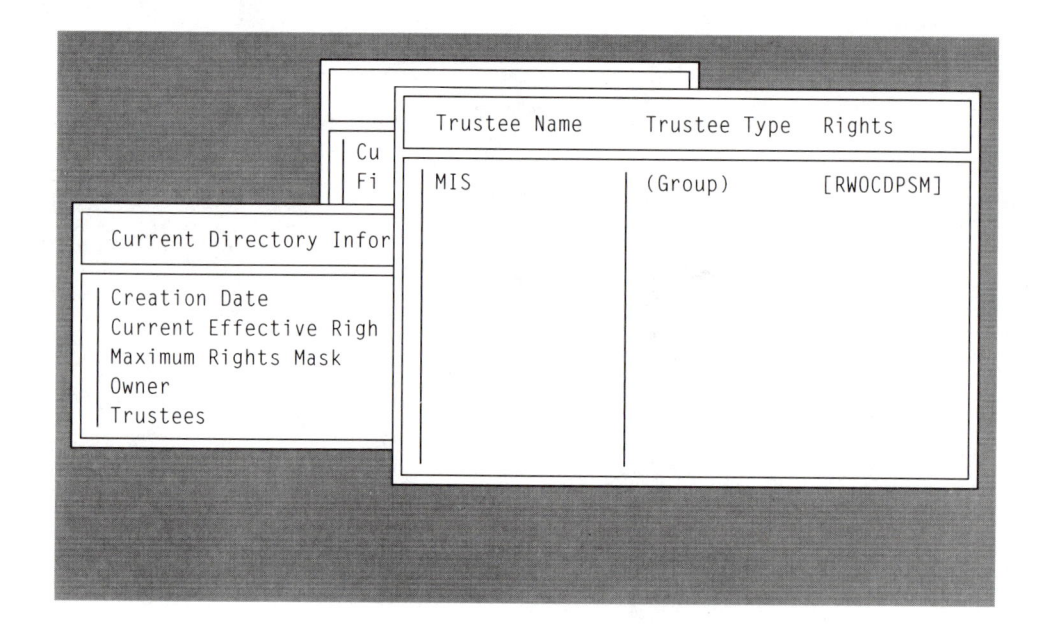

Trustee Name	Trustee Type	Rights
MIS	(Group)	[RWOCDPSM]

Current Directory Infor

Creation Date
Current Effective Righ
Maximum Rights Mask
Owner
Trustees

MENU UTILITIES REFERENCE

List a Directory's Files and Subdirectories (FILER)

> Include if user
>
> - Lists files and directories (all users except extreme novices should; Search right required to list files)
>
> - Lists files with operating system (not just in applications)

> Depending on your users' level of sophistication, you may also want to include the following note:

You must have the appropriate security privileges to list a directory's files. If you don't, no files are shown, although they may exist.

Action	**Display**
1. Access FILER.	FILER "Available Topics" menu
2. To list a directory's files, choose "File Information."	"Files" window (see next page)
3. To list a directory's subdirectories, choose "Subdirectory Information."	"Subdirectories" window (see next page)

NETWORK USER'S GUIDE   263

THE NETWARE 286 MANUAL MAKER

Sample "Files" window:

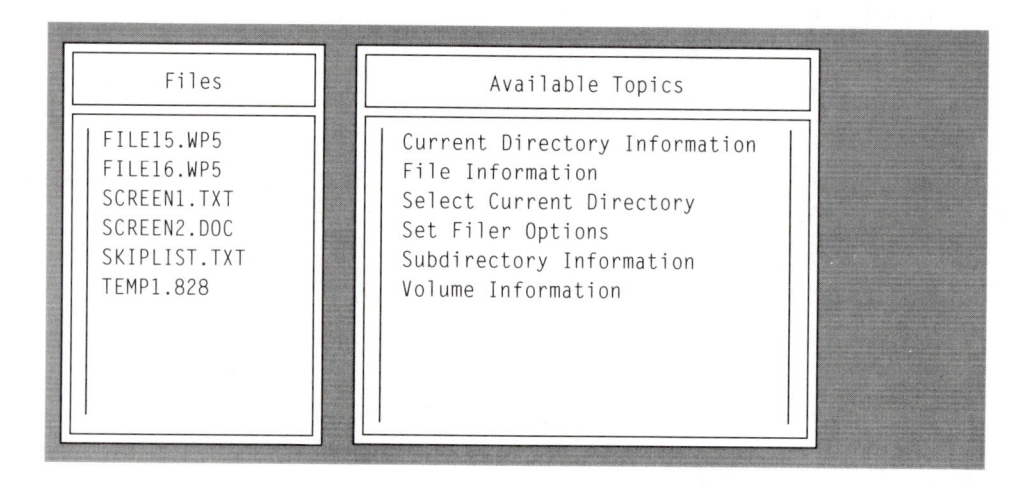

```
┌─────────────────────┐  ┌─────────────────────────────┐
│       Files         │  │      Available Topics       │
├─────────────────────┤  ├─────────────────────────────┤
│ FILE15.WP5          │  │ Current Directory Information│
│ FILE16.WP5          │  │ File Information            │
│ SCREEN1.TXT         │  │ Select Current Directory    │
│ SCREEN2.DOC         │  │ Set Filer Options           │
│ SKIPLIST.TXT        │  │ Subdirectory Information    │
│ TEMP1.828           │  │ Volume Information          │
│                     │  │                             │
└─────────────────────┘  └─────────────────────────────┘
```

Sample "Subdirectories" window:

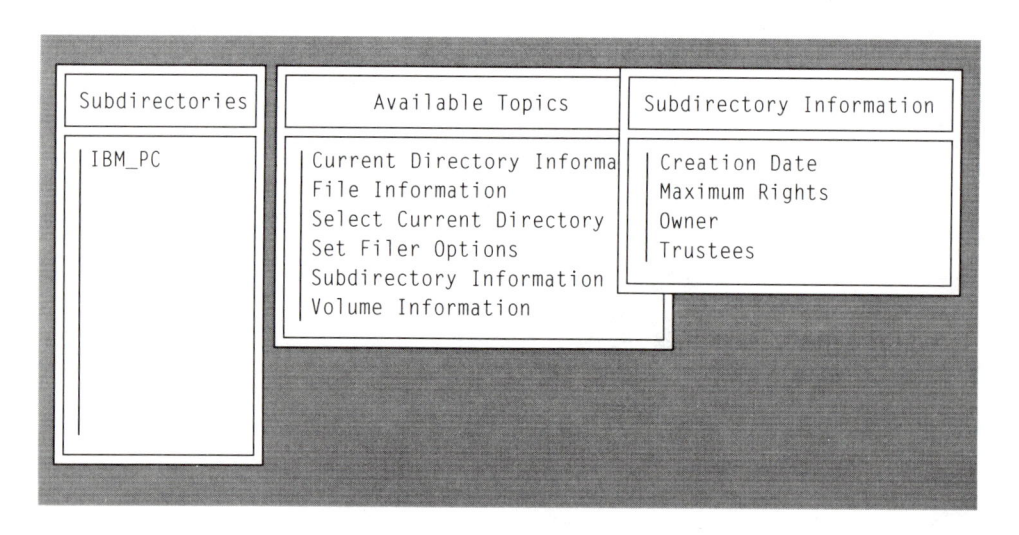

```
┌──────────────┐  ┌──────────────────────────┐ ┌────────────────────────┐
│Subdirectories│  │    Available Topics      │ │Subdirectory Information│
├──────────────┤  ├──────────────────────────┤ ├────────────────────────┤
│ IBM_PC       │  │ Current Directory Informa│ │ Creation Date          │
│              │  │ File Information         │ │ Maximum Rights         │
│              │  │ Select Current Directory │ │ Owner                  │
│              │  │ Set Filer Options        │ │ Trustees               │
│              │  │ Subdirectory Information │ └────────────────────────┘
│              │  │ Volume Information       │
│              │  └──────────────────────────┘
│              │
└──────────────┘
```

MENU UTILITIES REFERENCE

Delete a File (FILER)

> Include if user
>
> - Deletes files (requires Delete right)
>
> - Deletes files with operating system (not just in applications)

> Since users cannot delete files unless they have the Delete right in a directory, you may want to list the directories where the user has this right. You can use the following sample text to do so if you want.

On our network, you can delete files in the following directories:

<List the directories where the user has the Delete right here; refer to your master list of the user's rights throughout the directory tree if desired (see page 248 of the unmodified Manual Maker).>

Action	Display
1. Access FILER.	FILER "Available Topics" menu
2. Choose "File Information."	"Files" window
3. Highlight the file(s) you want to delete. (Use F5 to mark more than one.)	File(s) highlighted
4. Press DELETE.	"Delete file?" prompt
5. Answer "Yes."	File deleted

NETWORK USER'S GUIDE   265

THE NETWARE 286 MANUAL MAKER

Rename a File (FILER)

> Include if user
>
> • Renames files (probably only beneath home directory, while reorganizing; Modify right required)
>
> • Renames files with operating system (not just in applications)
>
> Rename a file.

> Since users cannot rename files unless they have the Modify right in a directory, you may want to list the directories where the user has this right. You can use the following sample text to do so if you want.

On our network, you can rename files in these directories:

<List the directories where the user has the Modify right here>

Action	Display
1. Access FILER.	FILER "Available Topics" menu
2. Choose "Directory Contents."	Directory's files and subdirectories
3. Highlight the file you want to delete.	File highlighted
4. Press MODIFY (F3).	"New Name" entry box
5. Type the file's new name.	

MENU UTILITIES REFERENCE

Copy a File (FILER)

> Include if user
>
> - Copies files (requires Read, Open, and Search rights in the source directory, and the Create right in the target directory)
>
> - Copies files with operating system (not just in applications)

Copy files between network directories and/or local drives or hard disks.

> Since users cannot copy files unless they have the appropriate rights, you may want to list the directories where the user has these rights. You can use the following sample text to do so if you want.

On our network, you can copy files to and from these directories.

Dirs. You Can Copy Files From	Dirs. You Can Copy Files To
<List the directories here— User must have Read, Open, and Search rights in them>	<List the directories here— User must have the Write and Create rights in them>

Action	Display
1. Access FILER.	FILER "Available Topics" menu
2. Choose "File Information."	"Files" window
3. Highlight the file you want to copy.	File highlighted

NETWORK USER'S GUIDE 267

THE NETWARE 286 MANUAL MAKER

4. Press ENTER.   Menu appears

5. Choose "Copy File."   "Destination Directory" entry box

6. Specify the directory you
   want to copy the files to, or
   press INSERT and choose
   sub-directories.

7. Press ENTER.   Destination File name:

8. Press ENTER to copy under
   the same name; type a new name
   rename the copy of the file.

See a File's Attributes (FILER)

> Include if user
>
> - Understands NetWare security attributes
>
> - Needs to see file attributes (usually while troubleshooting to find out why a certain task, such as opening a file, cannot be performed)
>
> Few users check attributes.

> Since users cannot view file attributes unless they have the Search and Parental rights in a directory, you may want to list the directories where the user has these rights. You can use the following sample text to do so if you want.

File attributes, along with rights, determine whether a file can be shared and whether it can be changed or only read.

On our network, you can view the attributes of files in the following directories:

<List the directories where the user has the Search and Parental rights here; refer to your master list of the user's rights throughout the directory tree if desired (see page 248 of the unmodified Manual Maker).>

THE NETWARE 286 MANUAL MAKER

Action	Display
1. Access FILER.	"Available Options" menu
2. Go to the parent directory of the directory whose files you want to view.	
3. Choose "File Information."	"Files" window
4. Highlight the file.	"File Information" window
5. Choose "Attributes."	"File Attributes" window

Sample "File Attributes" window:

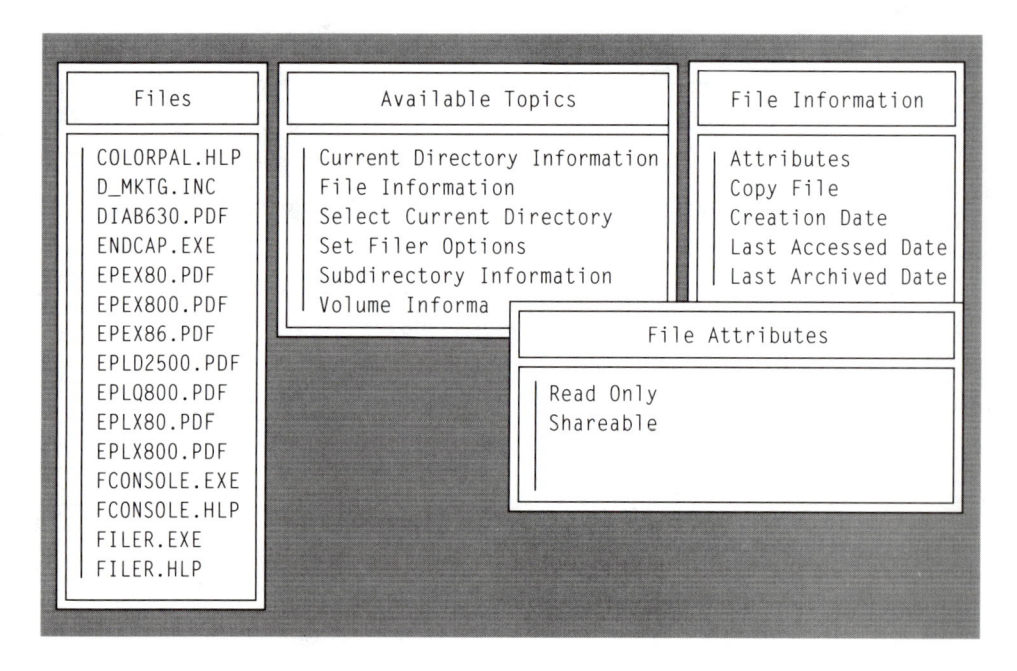

```
┌─────────────────┐ ┌──────────────────────────────┐ ┌──────────────────────┐
│      Files      │ │       Available Topics       │ │   File Information   │
├─────────────────┤ ├──────────────────────────────┤ ├──────────────────────┤
│ COLORPAL.HLP    │ │ Current Directory Information│ │ Attributes           │
│ D_MKTG.INC      │ │ File Information             │ │ Copy File            │
│ DIAB630.PDF     │ │ Select Current Directory     │ │ Creation Date        │
│ ENDCAP.EXE      │ │ Set Filer Options            │ │ Last Accessed Date   │
│ EPEX80.PDF      │ │ Subdirectory Information     │ │ Last Archived Date   │
│ EPEX800.PDF     │ │ Volume Informa ┌─────────────┴─────────────────┐
│ EPEX86.PDF      │ └────────────────┤        File Attributes        │
│ EPLD2500.PDF    │                  ├───────────────────────────────┤
│ EPLQ800.PDF     │                  │ Read Only                     │
│ EPLX80.PDF      │                  │ Shareable                     │
│ EPLX800.PDF     │                  │                               │
│ FCONSOLE.EXE    │                  │                               │
│ FCONSOLE.HLP    │                  └───────────────────────────────┘
│ FILER.EXE       │
│ FILER.HLP       │
└─────────────────┘
```

MENU UTILITIES REFERENCE

File Attributes List

Here are the most common file attributes.

Shareable—file can be opened by more than one user at a time
Non**S**hareable—file can only be opened by one user at a time
Read**O**nly—file can be read, but not changed
Read**W**rite—file can be changed
Normal—flags file Shareable, Read Write

THE NETWARE 286 MANUAL MAKER

Create a Directory (FILER)

> Include if user
>
> - Understands directory structures
>
> - Creates directory structures (usually under home directory; Create right required)

> Since users cannot create subdirectories beneath a directory unless they have the Create right in that directory, you may want to list the directories where the user has this right. You can use the following sample text to do so if you want.

On our network, you can create directories beneath these directories:

<List the directories where the user has the Create right here; refer to your master list of the user's rights throughout the directory tree if desired (see page 248 of the unmodified Manual Maker).>

Action	Display
1. Access FILER.	FILER "Available Topics" menu
2. Choose "Subdirectory Information."	"Subdirectories" window
3. Press INSERT.	"New subdirectory name:" entry box
4. Type the subdirectory's name.	
5. Press ENTER.	

MENU UTILITIES REFERENCE

Delete a Directory (FILER)

> Include if user
>
> - Understands directory structures
>
> - Deletes directories (usually under home directory, while reorganizing files; Delete right required)

Erase a directory.

> Since users cannot erase a directory unless they have the Delete right in its parent directory, you may want to list the directories where the user has this right. You can use the following sample text to do so if you want.

On our network, you can delete subdirectories beneath these directories:

<List the directories where the user has the Delete right here>

Action	**Display**
1. Access FILER.	FILER "Available Topics" menu
2. Choose "Subdirectory	"Subdirectories" window Information.
3. Highlight the directory you want to delete.	
4. Press DELETE.	"Delete Subdirectory?"
5. Answer "Yes."	

NETWORK USER'S GUIDE 273

THE NETWARE 286 MANUAL MAKER

Rename a Directory (FILER)

> Include if user
>
> - Renames directories (probably only beneath home directory, while reorganizing; Modify right required)
>
> - Renames directories with operating system (not just in applications)

Rename a directory.

> Since users cannot rename a directory unless they have the Modify right in the directory's parent directory, you may want to list the directories where the user has this right. You can use the following sample text to do so if you want.

On our network, you can rename subdirectories of these directories:

\<List the directories where the user has the Modify right here\>

Action	Display
1. Access FILER.	FILER "Available Topics" menu
2. Choose "Subdirectory Information".	"Subdirectories" window
3. Highlight the directory you want to rename.	
4. Press MODIFY (F3).	Entry Box
5. Type the directory's new name.	
6. Press ENTER.	Subdirectory renamed

MENU UTILITIES REFERENCE

Set FILER Options (FILER)

> Include if
>
> - You expect the user to work in FILER a lot
>
> - The user wants to specify how he or she works with FILER, or does selective directory and file lookups.
>
> Most users never do this task.

Action

1. Access FILER.

2. Choose "Set Filer Options."

Display

FILER "Available Topics" menu

Shown below.

Filer Option Settings

Confirm Deletions:
Confirm File Copies:
Confirm File Overwrites:

Directories Exclude Pattern:
Directory Include Patterns:

File Exclude Pattern:
File Include Pattern:

File Search Pattern:

NETWORK USER'S GUIDE   275

THE NETWARE 286 MANUAL MAKER

See Volume Information (FILER)

> Include if the user needs to see
>
> • How much directory space is left on a volume
>
> • How many directory entries are available on a volume
>
> (Only sophisticated users would understand this information. As supervisor, you should check this information often. However, nonadministrative users would probably check this information when troubleshooting to find out why a file cannot be saved, a directory cannot be created, or a directory cannot be mapped, since these operations involve directory space and directory entries.)

Action	Display
1. Access FILER.	FILER "Available Topics" menu
2. Choose "Volume Information."	Shown below.

Volume Information

Server Name:	LATE
Volume Name:	SYS
Volume Type:	fixed
Total Bytes:	
KBytes Available:	
Maximum Directory Entries:	
Directory Entries Available:	3,647

276   NETWORK USER'S GUIDE

MENU UTILITIES REFERENCE

List Print Queues (PCONSOLE)

> Include if user
>
> - Understands NetWare printing
>
> - Has reason to list print queues (usually done on the way to another task, such as printing files)

Action	Display
1. Access PCONSOLE.	PCONSOLE "Available Topics" menu
2. Choose "Print Queue Information."	"Print Queue Information" listing any print jobs currently in the queue

Sample "Print Queue Information" screen:

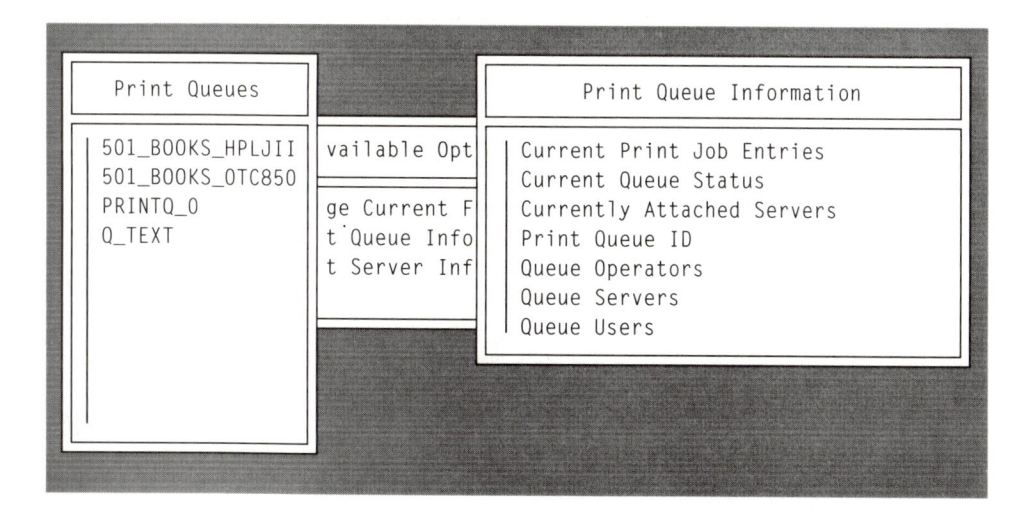

```
        Print Queues                           Print Queue Information

 501_BOOKS_HPLJII   vailable Opt    Current Print Job Entries
 501_BOOKS_OTC850                   Current Queue Status
 PRINTQ_0           ge Current F    Currently Attached Servers
 Q_TEXT             t Queue Info    Print Queue ID
                    t Server Inf    Queue Operators
                                    Queue Servers
                                    Queue Users
```

NETWORK USER'S GUIDE   277

THE NETWARE 286 MANUAL MAKER

List Print Jobs (PCONSOLE)

> Include only if the user
>
> - Understands NetWare printing
>
> - Has reason to look at all of the print jobs in a queue. (To look at print jobs this way, the user must know what queue[s] his or her print jobs go to. If you have more than one queue on your server, you may want to tell users which queues their print jobs go to.)

Action	Display
1. Access PCONSOLE.	PCONSOLE "Available Topics" menu
2. Choose "Print Queue Information."	Print queues
3. Choose the print queue whose jobs you want to view.	Print jobs in that queue

MENU UTILITIES REFERENCE

Sample print jobs screen:

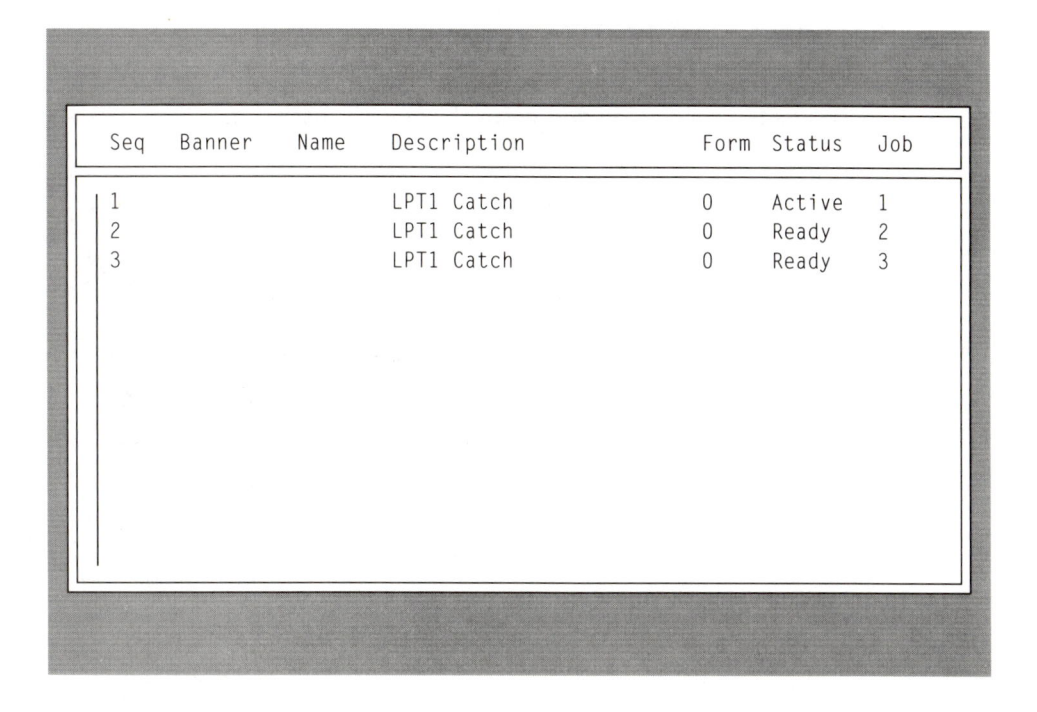

Seq	Banner	Name	Description	Form	Status	Job
1			LPT1 Catch	0	Active	1
2			LPT1 Catch	0	Ready	2
3			LPT1 Catch	0	Ready	3

NETWORK USER'S GUIDE 279

THE NETWARE 286 MANUAL MAKER

Print a file (PCONSOLE)

> Include if
>
> - User understands NetWare printing
>
> - User prints files created in non-network applications
>
> - You have not set up custom menus to be used for printing

> This method of printing is somewhat cumbersome, and requires the user to have a fairly good knowledge of how NetWare printing works. Unless you have trained users thoroughly in how network printing works, I recommend that you don't teach them how to print a file this way. Instead, create an interactive menu or batch file that prompts the user for the file he or she wants to print, then prints it with the NPRINT command line utility.

Action	Display
1. Access PCONSOLE.	PCONSOLE "Available Options" menu.
2. Choose "Print Queue Information" in the "Available Topics" menu.	"Print Queues" list
3. Choose the print queue you want to send the file to for printing.	"Print Queue Information" menu
4. Choose "Current Print Job Entries."	Current print job entries list (it may not have any entries in it)

MENU UTILITIES REFERENCE

5. Press INSERT. "Select Directory to Print From" box

6. Specify the directory you want to print from. In most cases, this is your current directory. (If not, press INSERT and choose subdirectories until you have specified the desired directory.)

   Directory path appears in box as you specify it

7. Press ENTER. "Available Files" list

8. Choose the file you want to print. To choose more than one, highlight each and press MARK (F5).

   Highlighted file(s)

9. Press ENTER. "Print Job Configurations" list

10. Choose the desired print job configuration.

    "New Print Job to be Submitted" form

11. Change print job parameters if you need to (see next page).

    Fields in form change according to what you specify

12. Press ESCAPE. "Save Changes" menu

13. Choose "Yes." Print job is inserted in queue

NETWORK USER'S GUIDE   281

THE NETWARE 286 MANUAL MAKER

Print Job Parameters

Here is an explanation of the print job parameters shown in the "New Print Job to be Submitted" screen in PCONSOLE. Some of these parameters cannot be changed, and there are some that you won't want to change when you submit a print job initially. The parameters you might change are marked with an asterisk.

Print Job. This field is blank initially, since the print job hasn't actually been submitted yet.

Client. Your username.

Description. The file's name—unless you have highlighted multiple files, in which case it says "(Filename)."

Status. This field is blank initially, since the print job hasn't actually been submitted yet.

User Hold. Should read "No" initially. (Can be changed to "Yes" to hold the print job later.)

Operator Hold. Should read "No" initially. (Print queue operators can change to "Yes" to hold the print job later.)

Service Sequence. This field is blank initially, since the print job hasn't actually been submitted yet. Once the job is in the print queue, the number in this field shows the job's position in the queue.

Job Entry Date and Job Entry Time. These two fields show when the job was put in the print queue.

*Number of copies. How many copies to print.

*File Contents. Text or Byte Stream. "Text" tells the printer to translate tabs to spaces; "Byte Stream" tells the printer to send all characters directly to the printer without translation. If you are printing from an application that does its own formatting

282   NETWORK USER'S GUIDE

MENU UTILITIES REFERENCE

(this is usually the case), use Byte Stream. This is especially true if you are printing graphics, fonts, or any other file that has extensive printing commands.

***Tab size.** The number of spaces the tabs should be converted to in your document, if you selected "Text."

***Suppress Form Feed.** Change this field to "Yes" if your job prints with an extra blank page at the end.

***Notify when done.** Specify "Yes" if you want to be told when your job has printed.

***Target server.** The print server that services the job. (To list the available print servers, press ENTER. Then choose the server you want.)

***Form.** The type of paper to print the job on. (To list the available forms, press ENTER. Then choose the form you want.)

***Print banner.** Whether you want a banner page to print. A print banner is an extra sheet of paper that prints before the job and identifies the job name and who printed the job.

***Name.** The username you want to print on the print banner. Identifies who printed the job.

***Banner name.** The filename you want to print on the print banner. Identifies the job itself.

***Defer printing.** Whether to print the job at a later time. (You must be a print queue operator to do this.)

***Target date.** If you have deferred printing, the date you want your job to print. (You must be a print queue operator to do this.)

***Target time.** If you have deferred printing, the time you want your job to print.

NETWORK USER'S GUIDE   283

THE NETWARE 286 MANUAL MAKER

Delete a Print Job (PCONSOLE)

> Include if user
>
> • Understands NetWare printing
>
> • Deletes print jobs with the operating system (not in applications only)

Unless you are a print queue operator, you can only delete your own print jobs.

> If the user is a print queue operator for any queues, you may want to list those queues here.

You are a print queue operator for <list the queues here>. This means you can delete other users' print jobs in these queues.

Action	Display
1. Access PCONSOLE.	PCONSOLE "Available Options" menu
2. Choose "Print Queue Information" in the "Available Topics" menu.	"Print Queues" list
3. Choose the print queue that contains the job you want to delete.	"Print Queue Information" menu
4. Choose "Current Print Job Entries."	Current print job entries list
5. Highlight the job you want to delete and press DELETE.	"Delete Queue Entry" prompt
6. Choose "Yes."	

284   NETWORK USER'S GUIDE

MENU UTILITIES REFERENCE

Change Order of Print Jobs (PCONSOLE)

> Include if user
>
> - Is a print queue operator.
>
> If you include this task, you should also tell the user which queue(s) he or she is an operator for. Sample text follows.

You can only change the order of print jobs in a print queue if you are an operator for that print queue. You are a print queue operator for the following print queues:

<List print queues here>

THE NETWARE 286 MANUAL MAKER

Action

1. Access PCONSOLE.

2. Choose "Print Queue Information"

3. Choose the print queue that contains the job(s) whose order you want to change.

4. Choose "Current Print Job Entries."

5. Choose the print job you want to move.

6. Highlight the "Server Sequence" parameter.

7. Type the number of the position you want to move the job to. (For example, to move a job to the top of the queue, you'd type the number one.)

Display

PCONSOLE "Available Options" menu

"Print Queues" list

"Print Queue Information" menu

Current print job entries list

MENU UTILITIES REFERENCE

Place a Hold on a Print Job (PCONSOLE)

> Include if user
>
> • Understands NetWare printing

You can only hold your own print jobs.

> Regular users can only place a hold on their own print jobs; print queue operators can place a hold on any print job in the queue. Also, before users can hold print jobs as explained here, they must know which queues the jobs are in.

Action

Display

1. Access PCONSOLE.   PCONSOLE "Available Options" menu.

2. Choose "Print Queue Information."   "Print Queues" list

3. Choose the print queue that   "Print Queue Information" menu
   contains the job(s) whose order you
   want to change.

4. Choose "Current Print Job Entries."   Current print job entries list

5. Choose the print job you
   want to place a hold on.

6. Highlight the "User Hold" field.

7. Type "Y" for yes.

8. Press ESCAPE.

NETWORK USER'S GUIDE   287

THE NETWARE 286 MANUAL MAKER

See a Print Queue's Status (PCONSOLE)

> Include this task if
>
> - The user understands NetWare printing thoroughly
>
> - You expect the user to check whether a queue is active (probably when troubleshooting to figure out why a job isn't printing)

A print queue's status shows if the queue is active or inactive.

Action	Display
1. Access PCONSOLE.	PCONSOLE "Available Options" menu
2. Choose "Print Queue Information."	"Print Queues" list
3. Choose the print queue whose status you want to see.	"Print Queue Information" menu
4. Choose "Current Queue Status."	

MENU UTILITIES REFERENCE

Sample "Current Queue Status" screen:

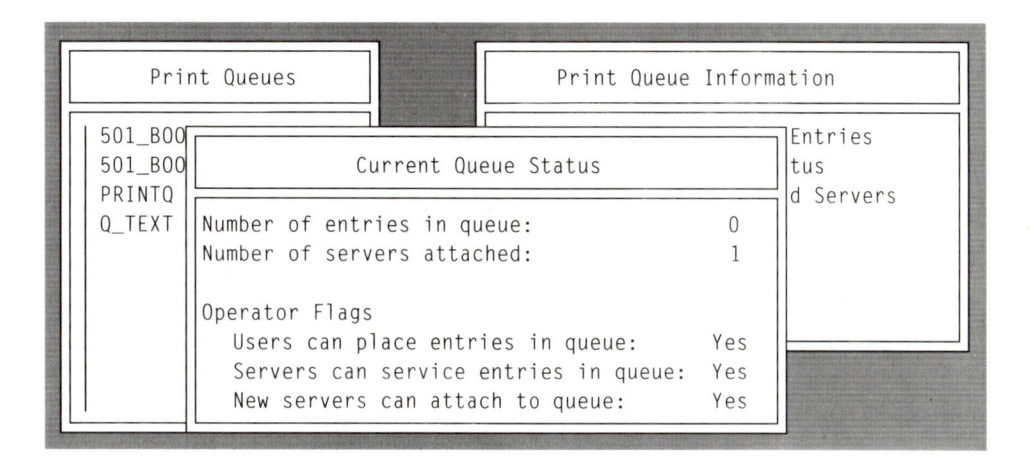

```
┌─────────────────────────┐  ┌──────────────────────────────┐
│      Print Queues       │  │    Print Queue Information   │
├─────────────────────────┤  ├──────────────────────────────┤
│ 501_B00┌─────────────────────────────────────────┐ Entries│
│ 501_B00│          Current Queue Status           │ tus    │
│ PRINTQ │                                         │ d Servers
│ Q_TEXT │ Number of entries in queue:         0   │        │
│        │ Number of servers attached:         1   │        │
│        │                                         │        │
│        │ Operator Flags                          │        │
│        │   Users can place entries in queue: Yes │        │
│        │   Servers can service entries in queue: Yes      │
│        │   New servers can attach to queue:  Yes │        │
│        └─────────────────────────────────────────┘        │
└─────────────────────────┘                                 
```

THE NETWARE 286 MANUAL MAKER

Change Your Current Server (SESSION)

> Include if
>
> - Network has more than one file server
>
> - User has an account on more than one of those servers

Action

1. Access SESSION.

2. Choose "Change Current Server."

3. Choose the file server you want to log in to.

Display

SESSION "Available Topics" menu

File servers and usernames

MENU UTILITIES REFERENCE

See/Set Drive Mappings (SESSION)

> Include if user
>
> - Understands directory structures
>
> - Understands drive mappings

> Drive mappings are usually created with the MAP command and saved in login scripts so that they are executed every time a user logs in. Drive mappings created in SESSION cannot be saved in login scripts, so drive mappings created here only last the duration of a login session.

Action	Display
1. Access SESSION.	SESSION "Available Topics" menu
2. Choose "Drive Mappings."	"Current Drive Mappings" list

To add a drive mapping, continue with the following steps.

Action	Display
3. Press INSERT.	"Drive:" prompt with next available drive letter displayed
4. Press ENTER.	"Select Directory" box
5. Press INSERT and choose subdirectories until you have specified the directory you want to map the drive to.	
6. Press ESCAPE.	"Select Directory" box
7. Press ENTER.	"Current Drive Mappings" with drive mapping added

NETWORK USER'S GUIDE   291

THE NETWARE 286 MANUAL MAKER

Send a Message to a Group (SESSION)

> Include if user
>
> - Sends short messages to other users at the command line

> It is much faster to send messages with the SEND command than with SESSION. For this reason, I don't recommend SESSION unless you want your users to work exclusively with menu utilities.

Action	Display
1. Access SESSION.	SESSION "Available Topics" menu
2. Choose "Group List."	"Group List"
3. Choose the group you want to send a message to.	"Message:" entry box
4. Type the message and press ENTER.	The message is sent to members of the group

MENU UTILITIES REFERENCE

See/Set Search Drive Mappings (SESSION)

> Include if user
>
> - Understands directory structures
>
> - Understands search drive mappings

> Search drive mappings are usually created with the MAP command and saved in login scripts so that they are executed every time a user logs in. Search drive mappings created in SESSION cannot be saved in login scripts, so those created here only last the duration of a login session.

NETWORK USER'S GUIDE   293

THE NETWARE 286 MANUAL MAKER

Action   **Display**

1. Access SESSION.   SESSION "Available Topics" menu

2. Choose "Search Mappings."   "Current Search Mappings" list

To add a search drive mapping, continue with the following steps.

3. Press INSERT.   "Search Drive Number:" prompt with
                                                         next available drive number displayed

4. Press ENTER.   "Select Directory" box

5. Press INSERT and choose
   subdirectories until you have
   specified the directory you
   want to map the search drive to.

6. Press ESCAPE.   "Select Directory" box

7. Press ENTER.   "Current Search Mappings" with new
                                                         search drive mapping added.

MENU UTILITIES REFERENCE

Select Default Drive (SESSION)

> Include if user
>
> - Understands how drive mappings work
>
> - Uses drive mappings to move around in the directory structure
>
> I don't recommend teaching users how to do this with SESSION; it is much easier to choose the default drive at the command line.

Action

1. Access SESSION.

2. Choose "Select Default Drive."

3. Choose the drive you want to make your current drive.

Display

SESSION "Available Topics" menu

"Select Default Drive" list

"Available Topics" menu

THE NETWARE 286 MANUAL MAKER

Send a Message to a User (SESSION)

> Include if user
>
> - Sends short messages to other users at the command line

> It is much faster to send messages with the SEND command than with SESSION. For this reason, I don't recommend teaching users how to send messages with SESSION.

Action	Display
1. Access SESSION.	SESSION "Available Topics" menu
2. Choose "User List."	Current Users Station
3. Choose the user(s) you want to send a message to.	If you chose one user: "Message:" entry box
	If you chose multiple users: "Available Options" menu
4. If you chose multiple users, choose "Send Message."	"Message:" entry box
5. Type the message and press ENTER.	The message is sent to the user(s).

296 NETWORK USER'S GUIDE

MENU UTILITIES REFERENCE

SYSCON USER TASKS

> Only the SYSCON tasks that non-administrative users would be likely to perform are included here. These tasks are found under the "Change Current Server," "Group Information," and "User Information" options in the SYSCON main menu. Tasks included under the "Accounting," "File Server Information," and "Supervisor Options" menu options are not included in this chapter, because most users wouldn't be concerned with tasks listed under them.

THE NETWARE 286 MANUAL MAKER

Change Your Current Server (SYSCON)

> Include if
>
> - Network has more than one file server
>
> - User has an account on more than one of those servers

Action

1. Access SYSCON.

2. Choose "Change Current Server."

3. Press INSERT.

4. Choose the file server you want to log in to.

5. Type your username and password, then press ENTER.

Display

SYSCON "Available Topics" menu

File servers and usernames

MENU UTILITIES REFERENCE

List Groups (SYSCON)

> Include if user
>
> - Understands NetWare security very well (enough to know that membership in a group gives him or her the same trustee rights as the group. However, for this purpose, it is better to use the SYSCON "User Information" option to list the groups the user belongs to than to use this option to list all the groups on the server)
>
> - Sends messages to groups with the SEND command and wants to list the groups that exist on the server, along with the members of each group. (If the user uses SESSION to send messages, groups are listed as part of the process; however, you cannot list group members in SESSION)

Generally, groups are a tool for supervisors to use in setting up the server efficiently. Most users won't have a lot to do with groups.

THE NETWARE 286 MANUAL MAKER

Action

1. Access SYSCON.

2. Choose "Group Information."

Sample "Group Names" list:

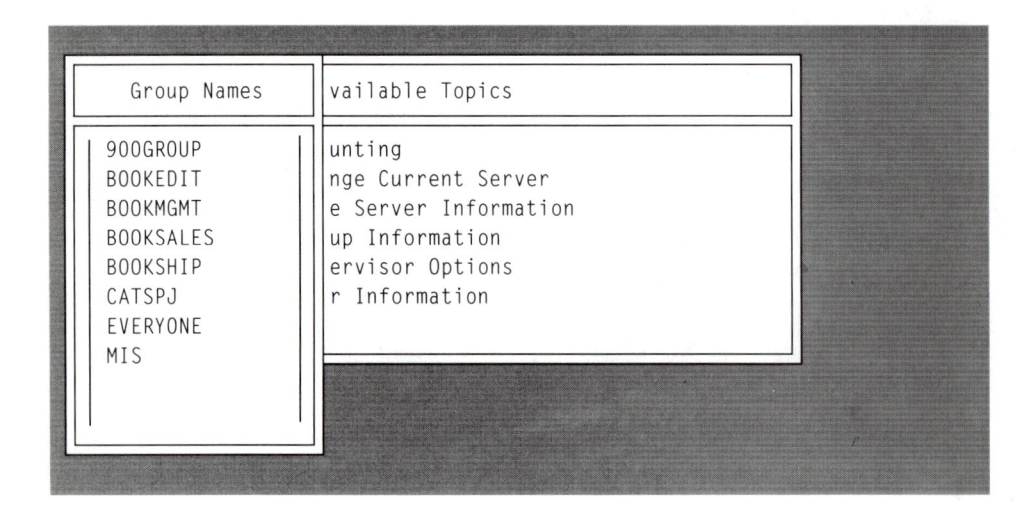

Display

SYSCON "Available Topics" menu

"Group Names" list

```
  Group Names      vailable Topics
  900GROUP         unting
  BOOKEDIT         nge Current Server
  BOOKMGMT         e Server Information
  BOOKSALES        up Information
  BOOKSHIP         ervisor Options
  CATSPJ           r Information
  EVERYONE
  MIS
```

MENU UTILITIES REFERENCE

See Group's Full Name (SYSCON)

> The ability to give a group a full name is meant mainly as a tool for supervisors (you can look up a group's full name if you need to jog your memory). The average user has little need to do this.

Action

Display

1. Access SYSCON.

   SYSCON "Available Topics" menu

2. Choose "Group Information."

   "Group Names" list

3. Choose the appropriate group.

   "Group Information" menu

4. Choose "Full Name."

   Group's full name

   If you belong to the group, you can also see the group's ID number and trustee rights.

NETWORK USER'S GUIDE   301

THE NETWARE 286 MANUAL MAKER

See Members of Group (SYSCON)

> Include if user
>
> - Sends messages to groups, and wants to check who is in a group.
>
> - Understands security well enough to know that being a member of a group gives him or her the same trustee rights as the group has, and thus wants to see if he or she is in a group. (However, both the SYSCON "User Information" option and the WHOAMI /G command are better for this purpose.)
>
> - Uses groups to assign security

Action	Display
1. Access SYSCON.	SYSCON "Available Topics" menu
2. Choose "Group Information."	Group menu
3. Choose the appropriate group.	"Group Information" menu
4. Choose "Member List."	Group members
	If you belong to the group, you can also see the group's ID number and trustee rights.

MENU UTILITIES REFERENCE

Sample "Group members" screen:

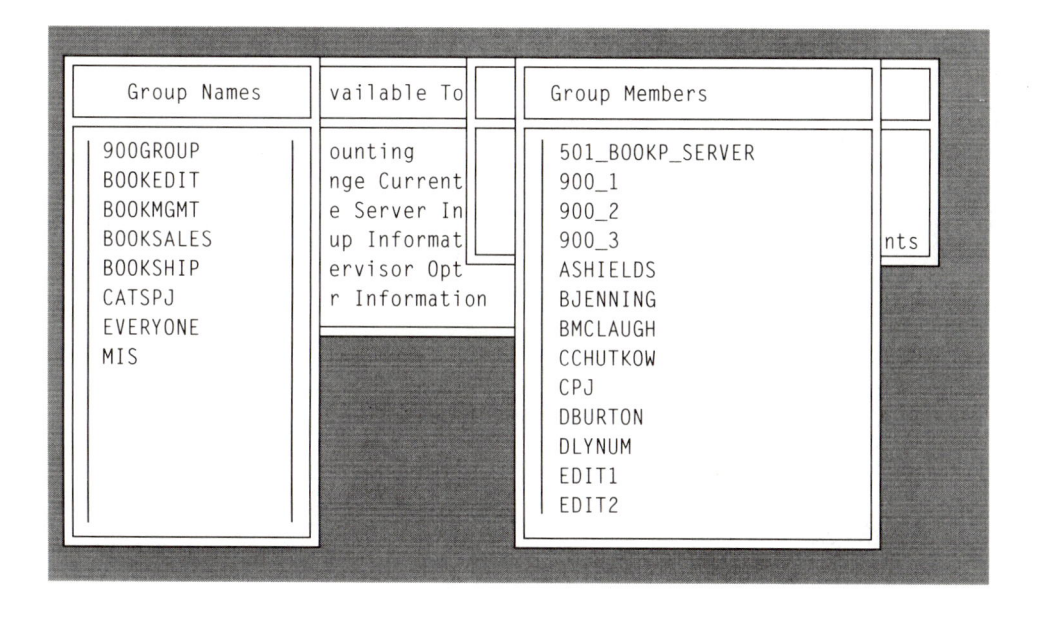

```
┌─────────────────┐ ┌─────────────┐
│  Group Names    │ │vailable To  │      ┌──────────────────┐
├─────────────────┤ ├─────────────┤      │  Group Members   │
│ 900GROUP        │ │ounting      │      ├──────────────────┤
│ BOOKEDIT        │ │nge Current  │      │ 501_BOOKP_SERVER │
│ BOOKMGMT        │ │e Server In  │      │ 900_1            │
│ BOOKSALES       │ │up Informat  │      │ 900_2            │    nts
│ BOOKSHIP        │ │ervisor Opt  │      │ 900_3            │
│ CATSPJ          │ │r Information│      │ ASHIELDS         │
│ EVERYONE        │ └─────────────┘      │ BJENNING         │
│ MIS             │                      │ BMCLAUGH         │
│                 │                      │ CCHUTKOW         │
│                 │                      │ CPJ              │
│                 │                      │ DBURTON          │
│                 │                      │ DLYNUM           │
│                 │                      │ EDIT1            │
│                 │                      │ EDIT2            │
└─────────────────┘                      └──────────────────┘
```

NETWORK USER'S GUIDE   303

THE NETWARE 286 MANUAL MAKER

See Trustee Assignments (Groups) (SYSCON)

> Include if user
>
> - Has the Parental right in any directories
>
> - Knows about NetWare security (only users with a very thorough understanding of NetWare security—including security rights, effective rights, trustee rights, and maximum rights masks—would ever want to list groups' trustee assignments. Users would also have to understand that all members of a group have the same trustee rights as that group.)

These are the directories where the group has been given direct security privileges.

Action	Display
1. Access SYSCON.	SYSCON "Available Topics" menu
2. Choose "Group Information."	Group menu
3. Choose the appropriate group.	"Group Information" menu
4. Choose "Trustee Directory Assignments" screen	"Trustee Directory Assignments."

See sample "Trustee Directory Assignments" screen, next page.

MENU UTILITIES REFERENCE

Sample "Trustee Directory Assignments" screen:

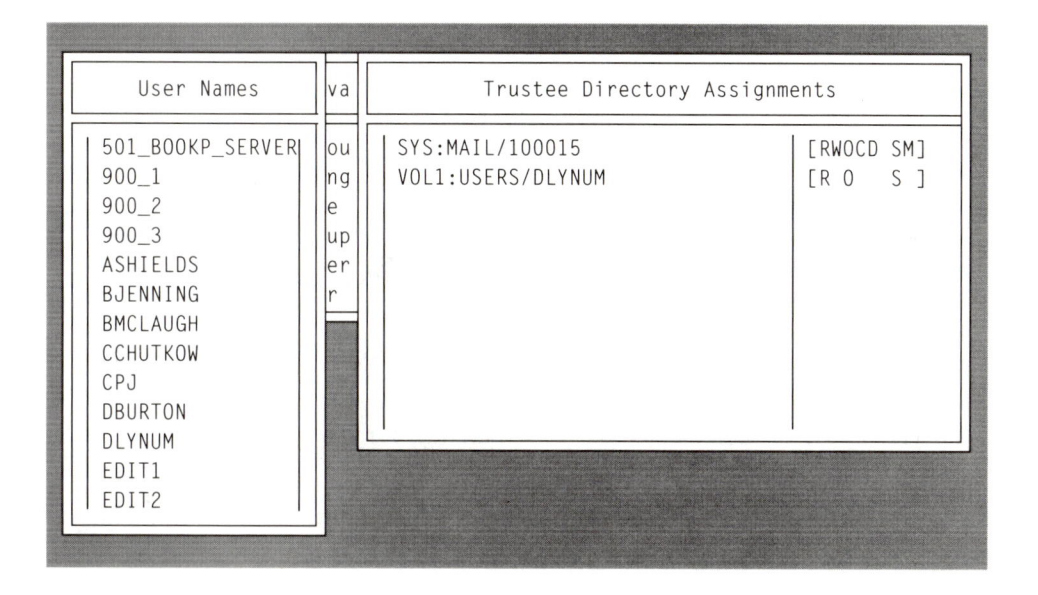

```
┌─────────────────────┬──┬──────────────────────────────────────────┐
│    User Names       │va│      Trustee Directory Assignments       │
├─────────────────────┤  ├──────────────────────────────────────────┤
│ 501_BOOKP_SERVER    │ou│  SYS:MAIL/100015           [RWOCD SM]    │
│ 900_1               │ng│  VOL1:USERS/DLYNUM         [R O    S ]   │
│ 900_2               │e │                                          │
│ 900_3               │up│                                          │
│ ASHIELDS            │er│                                          │
│ BJENNING            │r │                                          │
│ BMCLAUGH            │  │                                          │
│ CCHUTKOW            │  │                                          │
│ CPJ                 │  │                                          │
│ DBURTON             │  │                                          │
│ DLYNUM              │  │                                          │
│ EDIT1               │  │                                          │
│ EDIT2               │  │                                          │
└─────────────────────┴──┴──────────────────────────────────────────┘
```

THE NETWARE 286 MANUAL MAKER

> A brief explanation of the NetWare security rights is contained in the following table. You may want to include it here for users' convenience.

Here is a brief explanation of the NetWare security rights.

Letter	Right	Allows you to
R	Read	See the contents of files and execute application files
W	Write	Change the contents of existing files
O	Open	Open files for use
C	Create	Create files and directories
D	Delete	Delete files and directories
P	Parental	Assign security
S	Search	List files in a directory
M	Modify	Change the security attributes of files and directories

306   NETWORK USER'S GUIDE

MENU UTILITIES REFERENCE

See Trustee Assignments (Your Own) (SYSCON)

> Include if user
>
> - Knows about NetWare security (users would generally check trustee assignments when troubleshooting to figure out how their effective rights were determined. Only users with a very thorough understanding of NetWare security—including security rights, effective rights, trustee rights, and maximum rights masks—would ever do this.)

These are the directories where you have been given direct security privileges.

Action	Display
1. Access SYSCON.	SYSCON "Available Topics" menu
2. Choose "User Information."	"User Names" list
3. Choose your name.	"User Information" menu
4. Choose "Trustee Directory Assignments."	"Trustee Directory Assignments" shown

THE NETWARE 286 MANUAL MAKER

Sample "Trustee Directory Assignments" screen:

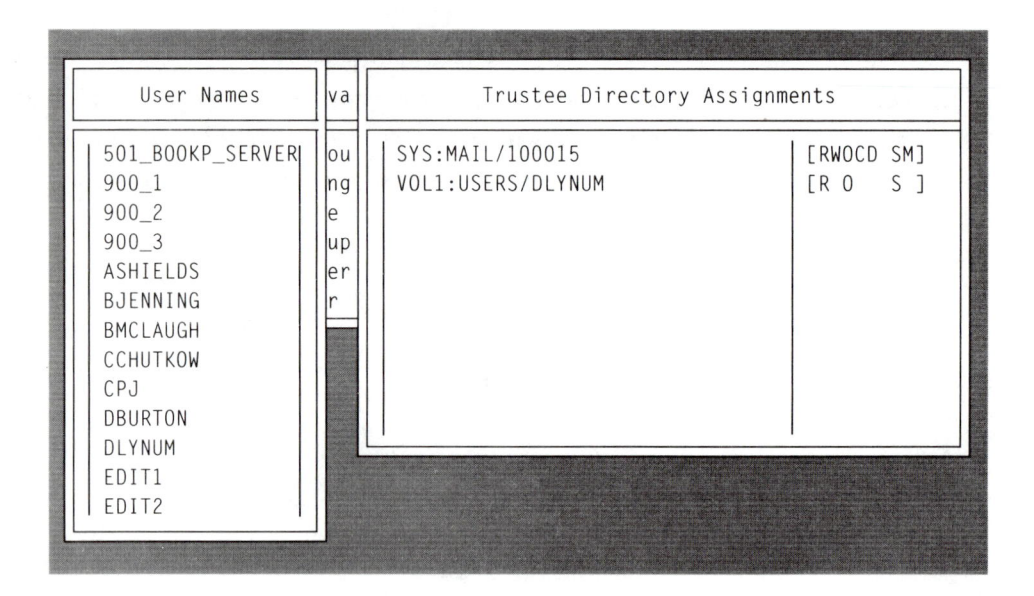

```
┌─────────────────┬───┬──────────────────────────────────────┐
│   User Names    │va │      Trustee Directory Assignments   │
├─────────────────┤   ├──────────────────────────────────────┤
│ 501_BOOKP_SERVER│ou │ SYS:MAIL/100015          [RWOCD SM]  │
│ 900_1           │ng │ VOL1:USERS/DLYNUM        [R O    S]  │
│ 900_2           │e  │                                      │
│ 900_3           │up │                                      │
│ ASHIELDS        │er │                                      │
│ BJENNING        │r  │                                      │
│ BMCLAUGH        │   │                                      │
│ CCHUTKOW        │   │                                      │
│ CPJ             │   │                                      │
│ DBURTON         │   │                                      │
│ DLYNUM          │   │                                      │
│ EDIT1           │   │                                      │
│ EDIT2           │   │                                      │
└─────────────────┴───┴──────────────────────────────────────┘
```

> A brief explanation of the NetWare security rights is contained in the following table. You may want to include it here for users' convenience.

308   NETWORK USER'S GUIDE

MENU UTILITIES REFERENCE

Here is a brief explanation of the NetWare security rights.

Letter	Right	Allows you to
R	Read	See the contents of files and execute application files
W	Write	Change the contents of existing files
O	Open	Open files for use
C	Create	Create files and directories
D	Delete	Delete files and directories
P	Parental	Assign security
S	Search	List files in a directory
M	Modify	Change the security attributes of files and directories

THE NETWARE 286 MANUAL MAKER

See Your Account Balance (SYSCON)

> Include if
>
> - Accounting is installed on the file server
>
> - You have established an account balance for the user

Your account balance determines the amount of network resources available to you. If there is a limit and you go below it, you are locked out of the system.

Action	**Display**
1. Access SYSCON.	SYSCON "Available Topics" menu
2. Choose "User Information."	"User Names" list
3. Choose your name.	"User Information" menu
4. Choose "Account Balance."	"Account Balance" display

Sample "Account Balance" display:

Account Balance For User CHRIS

Account Balance: 10000
Allow Unlimited Credit: No
Low Balance Limit: 50

---

310   NETWORK USER'S GUIDE

MENU UTILITIES REFERENCE

See Your Account Restrictions (SYSCON)

> Include if
>
> - You have established account restrictions for the user (even if you don't show users how to see their account restrictions, you should tell them what their restrictions are and what they mean.)

Account restrictions affect your ability to log in and control how you work with your password.

Action	Display
1. Access SYSCON.	SYSCON "Available Topics" menu
2. Choose "User Information."	"User Names" list
3. Choose your name.	"User Information" menu
4. Choose "Account Restrictions."	"Account Restrictions" display

THE NETWARE 286 MANUAL MAKER

Sample "Account Restrictions" display:

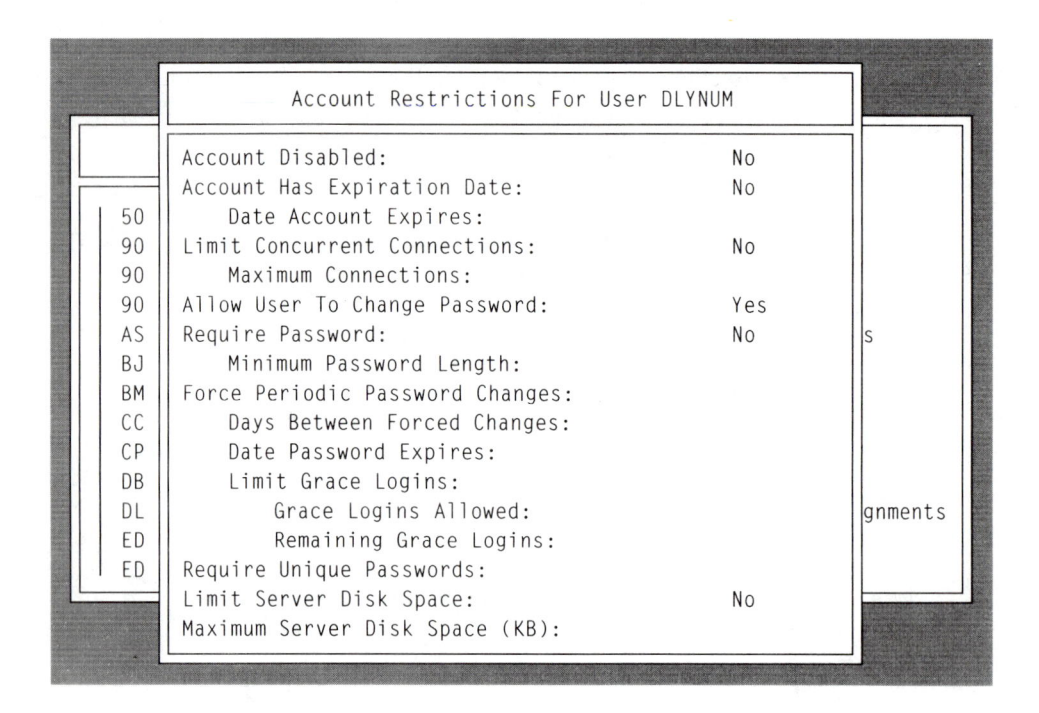

```
┌─────────────────────────────────────────────────────────┐
│      ┌──────────────────────────────────────────────┐   │
│      │      Account Restrictions For User DLYNUM    │   │
│  ┌───┤                                              ├───│
│  │   │ Account Disabled:                      No    │   │
│  │ 50│ Account Has Expiration Date:           No    │   │
│  │ 90│     Date Account Expires:                    │   │
│  │ 90│ Limit Concurrent Connections:          No    │   │
│  │ 90│     Maximum Connections:                     │   │
│  │ AS│ Allow User To Change Password:         Yes   │   │
│  │ BJ│ Require Password:                      No    │ s │
│  │ BM│     Minimum Password Length:                 │   │
│  │ CC│ Force Periodic Password Changes:             │   │
│  │ CP│     Days Between Forced Changes:             │   │
│  │ DB│     Date Password Expires:                   │   │
│  │ DL│     Limit Grace Logins:                      │gnments│
│  │ ED│         Grace Logins Allowed:                │   │
│  │ ED│         Remaining Grace Logins:              │   │
│  │   │ Require Unique Passwords:                    │   │
│  │   │ Limit Server Disk Space:               No    │   │
│  │   │ Maximum Server Disk Space (KB):              │   │
│      └──────────────────────────────────────────────┘   │
└─────────────────────────────────────────────────────────┘
```

The "Account Restrictions" display is explained on the next page.

312 NETWORK USER'S GUIDE

MENU UTILITIES REFERENCE

Field	Meaning
Account Disabled	If your account is disabled, you cannot log in.
Account Has Expiration Date	If there is a date after which you can no longer log in.
Date Account Expires	The date after which you can no longer log in.
Limit Concurrent Connections	Whether the number of workstations you can be logged into at the same time is limited.
Maximum Connections	How many workstations you can be logged into at the same time.
Allow User to Change Password	Whether you can change your own password.
Require Password	Whether or not passwords are required on your system.
Minimum Password Length	Minimum number of characters that your password must be.
Force Periodic Password Changes	Whether or not you are required to change your password periodically.

THE NETWARE 286 MANUAL MAKER

Days Between Forced Changes	How often you must change your password.

Date Password Expires	The date when you must change your password next.

Limit Grace Logins	Whether you can log in after your old password has expired.

Grace Logins Allowed	How many times you can log in after your old password has expired.

Remaining Grace Logins	How many grace logins you have left.

Require Unique Passwords	Whether you can use a password more than once.

MENU UTILITIES REFERENCE

Change Your Password (SYSCON)

> All users need to change their passwords. The only reasons not to include this command are if
>
> - You are one of very few installations that don't require passwords
>
> - You force periodic password changes and are certain that users only change their passwords then

Here is how to change your password when it is not a forced change.

Action	Display
1. Access SYSCON.	SYSCON "Available Topics" menu
2. Choose "User Information."	"User Names" list
3. Choose your name.	"User Information" menu
4. Choose "Change Password."	"Enter Old Password" prompt
5. Type your old password and press ENTER.	"Enter New Password" prompt
6. Type your new password and press ENTER.	"Retype New Password" prompt
7. Re-type your new password and press ENTER.	Return to "User Information" menu.

NETWORK USER'S GUIDE

THE NETWARE 286 MANUAL MAKER

See Your Full Name (SYSCON)

> The ability to give a user a full name is meant mainly as a tool for supervisors (you can look up a user's full name if you need to jog your memory). The average user has little need to do this.

Action   **Display**

1. Access SYSCON.   SYSCON "Available Topics" menu

2. Choose "User Information."   "User Names" list

3. Choose your name.   "User Information" menu

4. Choose "Full Name."   Full name shown

See the Groups You Belong To (SYSCON)

> Include only if user
>
> - Understands NetWare security well enough to know that membership in a group gives them the same trustee rights as that group has.
>
> - Looks at his or her own security (if users look at their own security, it is important for them to know what groups they belong to, because many of their trustee assignments may be given to them via their group membership.)
>
> Most users won't need to know their group membership.

THE NETWARE 286 MANUAL MAKER

Action   **Display**

1. Access SYSCON.   SYSCON "Available Topics" menu

2. Choose "User Information."   "User Names" list

3. Choose your name.   "User Information" menu

4. Choose "Groups Belonged To."   "Groups Belonged To" list

    Sample "Groups Belonged To" list:

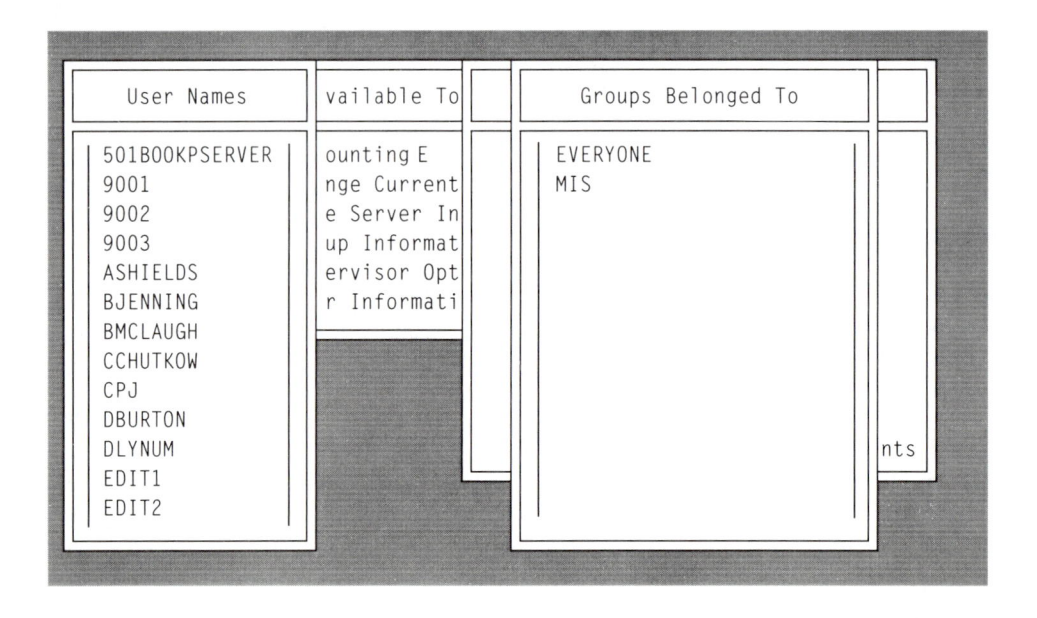

```
  User Names          vailable To        Groups Belonged To

  501BOOKPSERVER      ounting E          EVERYONE
  9001                nge Current        MIS
  9002                e Server In
  9003                up Informat
  ASHIELDS            ervisor Opt
  BJENNING            r Informati
  BMCLAUGH
  CCHUTKOW
  CPJ
  DBURTON
  DLYNUM                                                                nts
  EDIT1
  EDIT2
```

MENU UTILITIES REFERENCE

Access Your Login Script (SYSCON)

> Login scripts appeal mainly to curious users who have a technical bent. Login scripts are a great tool for users who know what they're doing; however, the ability to access a login script can be a double-edged sword, because users may change or delete vital information in their login scripts if they don't understand what is going on.
>
> I recommend that you decide whether to teach users about login scripts based on their general level of computer expertise, and your comfort level as far as letting them work in their own login scripts.
>
> NOTE: If you don't allow users to change their passwords, they won't be able to access their login scripts either. The login script option won't show in the user information menu. To prevent users from changing their passwords, put "No" in the "Allow User to Change Password" field of the Account Restrictions screen (see page 311 of the unmodified Manual Maker).

Login scripts contain instructions that are executed every time you log in. Your personal login script, what you see here, contains instructions that apply only to you.

Action	Display
1. Access SYSCON.	SYSCON "Available Topics" menu
2. Choose "User Information."	"User Names" list
3. Choose your name.	"User Information" menu

NETWORK USER'S GUIDE   319

THE NETWARE 286 MANUAL MAKER

See Security Equivalences (SYSCON)

> Include if user
>
> - Knows about NetWare security (only users with a very thorough understanding of NetWare security—including security rights, effective rights, trustee rights, and maximum rights masks—would ever check their security equivalences. In addition, users would have to understand that security equivalences give them the same rights as those that the users or groups they're equivalent to have directly.)

If you are security-equivalent to a user or group, you have the same security privileges as that user or group.

MENU UTILITIES REFERENCE

Action	Display
1. Access SYSCON.	SYSCON "Available Topics" menu
2. Choose "User Information."	"User Names" list
3. Choose your name.	"User Information" menu
4. Choose "Security Equivalences."	"Security Equivalences" list

Sample "Security Equivalences" list:

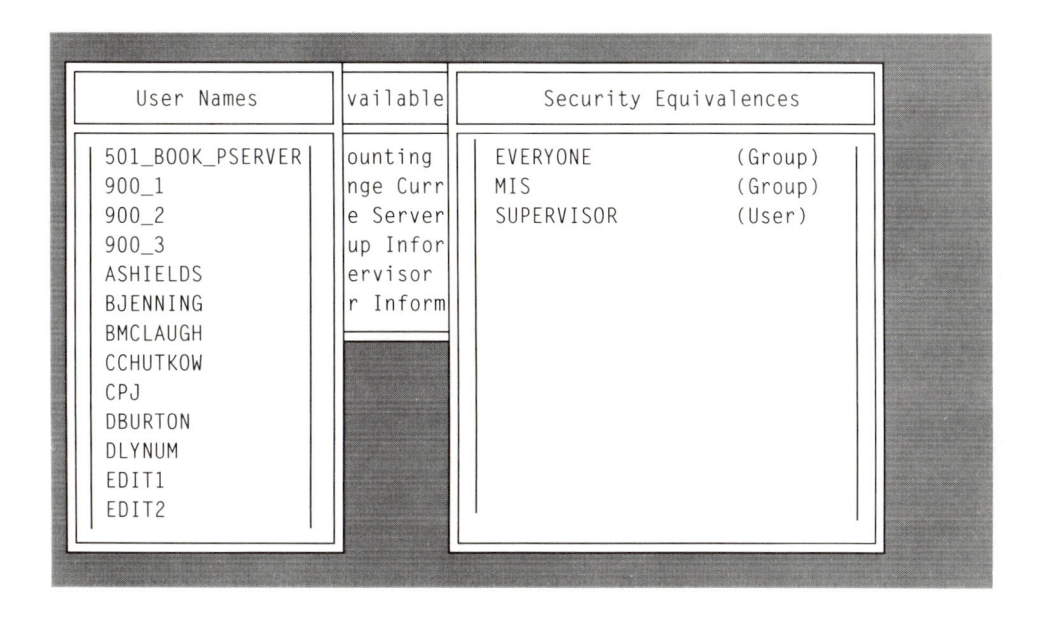

```
   User Names        vailable    Security Equivalences
 501_BOOK_PSERVER   ounting     EVERYONE      (Group)
 900_1              nge Curr    MIS           (Group)
 900_2              e Server    SUPERVISOR    (User)
 900_3              up Infor
 ASHIELDS           ervisor
 BJENNING           r Inform
 BMCLAUGH
 CCHUTKOW
 CPJ
 DBURTON
 DLYNUM
 EDIT1
 EDIT2
```

NETWORK USER'S GUIDE

THE NETWARE 286 MANUAL MAKER

See Station Restrictions (SYSCON)

> Include if user
>
> - Has station restrictions (even then, this information may not be useful, because it is presented in hexidecimal station addresses, not English-language descriptions).

These are the workstations you can log in from.

Action	Display
1. Access SYSCON.	SYSCON "Available Topics" menu
2. Choose "User Information."	"User Names" list
3. Choose your name.	"User Information" menu
4. Choose "Station Restrictions."	"Station Restrictions" list

MENU UTILITIES REFERENCE

Sample "Station Restrictions" list:

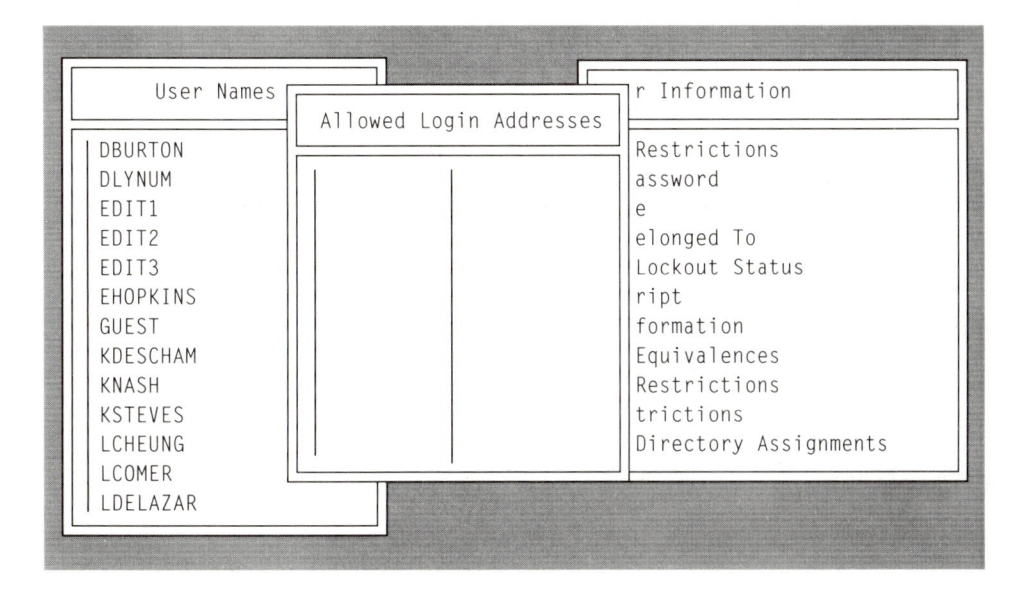

```
┌─────────────────────────────────────────────────────────────┐
│         User Names      ┌──────────────────────┐r Information │
│        ┌────────────────│Allowed Login Addresses│──────────┐  │
│        │ DBURTON        │                      │Restrictions│  │
│        │ DLYNUM         │          │           │assword    │  │
│        │ EDIT1          │          │           │e          │  │
│        │ EDIT2          │          │           │elonged To │  │
│        │ EDIT3          │          │           │Lockout Status│
│        │ EHOPKINS       │          │           │ript       │  │
│        │ GUEST          │          │           │formation  │  │
│        │ KDESCHAM       │          │           │Equivalences│ │
│        │ KNASH          │          │           │Restrictions│ │
│        │ KSTEVES        │          │           │trictions  │  │
│        │ LCHEUNG        │          │           │Directory Assignments│
│        │ LCOMER         └──────────────────────┘           │  │
│        │ LDELAZAR       │                                     │
│        └────────────────┘                                     │
└─────────────────────────────────────────────────────────────┘
```

NETWORK USER'S GUIDE   323

THE NETWARE 286 MANUAL MAKER

See Time Restrictions (SYSCON)

> Include if user
>
> - Has time restrictions.

These are the times you can use the network. You cannot log in during unauthorized time periods. If you log in during an unauthorized time period, you are automatically logged out.

Action   **Display**

1. Access SYSCON.   SYSCON "Available Topics" menu

2. Choose "User Information."   "User Names" list

3. Choose your name.   "User Information" menu

4. Choose "Time Restrictions."   See next page

MENU UTILITIES REFERENCE

```
┌─────────────────────────────────────────────────────────────┐
│              Allowed Login Times For User USERNAME          │
├─────────────────────────────────────────────────────────────┤
│                                                             │
│                     AM                     PM               │
│            1                 1 1 1                    1 1   │
│            2 1 2 3 4 5 6 7 8 9 0 1 2 1 2 3 4 5 6 7 8 9 0 1  │
│                                                             │
│  Sunday    ********************************************     │
│  Monday    ********************************************     │
│  Tuesday   ********************************************     │
│  Wednesday ********************************************     │
│  Thursday  ********************************************     │
│  Friday    ********************************************     │
│  Saturday  ********************************************     │
│                                                             │
│                               Sunday 12:00 am To 12:30 am   │
└─────────────────────────────────────────────────────────────┘
```

The time periods marked by asterisks are the times that you can use the network; the time periods that are not marked by asterisks indicate the times during which you cannot use the network.

THE NETWARE 286 MANUAL MAKER

See Trustee Directory Assignments (SYSCON)

> Include if user
>
> - Knows about NetWare security (most users would check their trustee assignments when troubleshooting to figure out how their effective rights were determined. Only users with a very thorough understanding of NetWare security—including security rights, effective rights, trustee rights, and maximum rights masks—would ever do this.)

These are the directories where you have been given direct security privileges.

Action

1. Access SYSCON.

2. Choose "User Information."

3. Choose your name.

4. Choose "Trustee Directory Assignments."

Display

SYSCON "Available Topics" menu

"User Names" list

"User Information" menu

"Trustee Directory Assignments" screen

326   NETWORK USER'S GUIDE

MENU UTILITIES REFERENCE

Sample "Trustee Directory Assignments" screen:

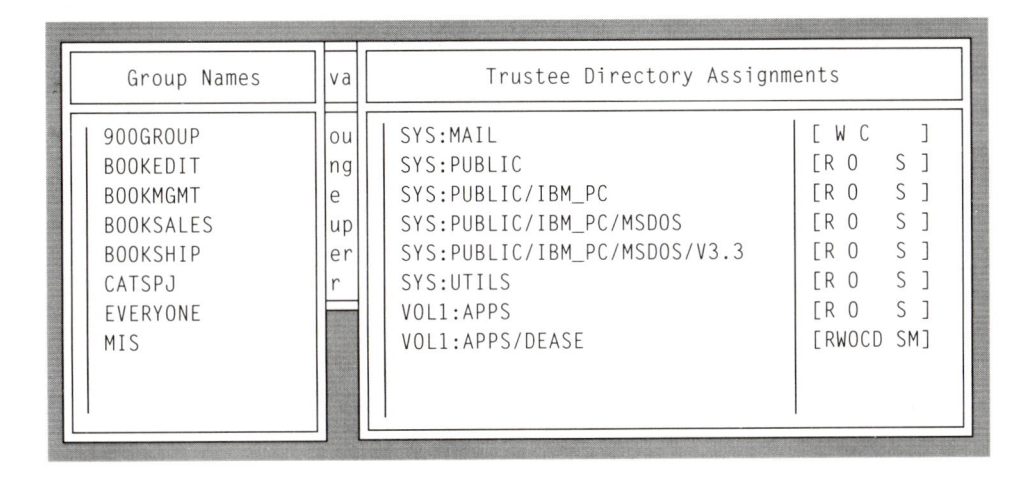

```
┌─────────────────────┬──┬──────────────────────────────────────────┐
│    Group Names      │va│      Trustee Directory Assignments       │
├─────────────────────┤  ├──────────────────────────────────────────┤
│  900GROUP           │ou│  SYS:MAIL                    [  W C    ] │
│  BOOKEDIT           │ng│  SYS:PUBLIC                  [R O    S ] │
│  BOOKMGMT           │e │  SYS:PUBLIC/IBM_PC           [R O    S ] │
│  BOOKSALES          │up│  SYS:PUBLIC/IBM_PC/MSDOS     [R O    S ] │
│  BOOKSHIP           │er│  SYS:PUBLIC/IBM_PC/MSDOS/V3.3 [R O   S ] │
│  CATSPJ             │r │  SYS:UTILS                   [R O    S ] │
│  EVERYONE           │  │  VOL1:APPS                   [R O    S ] │
│  MIS                │  │  VOL1:APPS/DEASE             [RWOCD SM] │
│                     │  │                                          │
└─────────────────────┴──┴──────────────────────────────────────────┘
```

NETWORK USER'S GUIDE   327

THE NETWARE 286 MANUAL MAKER

> A brief explanation of the NetWare security rights is contained in the following table. You may want to include it here for users' convenience.

Here is a brief explanation of the NetWare security rights.

Letter	Right	Allows you to
R	Read	See the contents of files and execute application files
W	Write	Change the contents of existing files
O	Open	Open files for use
C	Create	Create files and directories
D	Delete	Delete files and directories
P	Parental	Assign security
S	Search	List files in a directory
M	Modify	Change the security attributes of files and directories

CHAPTER OVERVIEW

Instructions for Final Formatting

The text for this boilerplate chapters is found in:
Format.WP (WordPerfect version)
Format.ASC (ASCII version)

This chapter provides directions for cleaning up and condensing the 286 manuals that you have just created to suit your users' needs. It begins with instructions for WordPerfect users and continues with instructions for users working in other formats, beginning on page 337.

CHAPTER 8

Instructions for Final Formatting

Formatting WordPerfect Files

To do the final formatting of Manual Maker files created in WordPerfect, complete these steps. (Note that keystrokes are contained in brackets or in indented lists.)

1. Retrieve all the files into one file.

   Unless your manuals will be very long (100+ pages), I recommend that you make them all one big file. This will make final formatting easier.

   To do so,

   A. Retrieve the first file you wish to include in your manual [SHIFT + F10].

   B. Save the file under a new name—preferably one which describes the manual you're making.

   C. Go to the very end of the file [HOME, HOME, down arrow key].

   D. Retrieve the second file into this file [SHIFT + F10, Yes].

   E. Continue with steps C and D until you have retrieved all the desired files into your manual file. Then save the file again.

THE NETWARE 286 MANUAL MAKER

2. Turn the Comments display off and fix the spacing.

   As noted in the introduction, the Comments contained throughout the text sometimes create some awkward spacing. You may also have created awkward page breaks, very short pages, lines of "orphan" text, etc., as you modified the chapters. Now is the time to fix these problems.
   A. Go to the very beginning of your text [HOME, HOME, up arrow key].

   B. Turn the Comments display off:
   SHIFT + F1
   Option 2 (Display)
   Option 6 (Edit Screen Options)
   Option 2 (Comments Display)
   No
   Press the Escape key three times

   With the Comments display off, you can see the pages as they will actually print. Page through the document and adjust the spacing as desired.

3. Make the page numbering sequential.

   Once you have fixed the spacing, you are ready to make sure that your pages will be numbered sequentially. To do so, complete these steps.

   A. Go to the very beginning of your text [HOME, HOME, up arrow key].

   B. If you wish to begin the manual on a page number other than 1, insert a new page number here at the beginning of the text.

   SHIFT + F8
   Option 2, Page

INSTRUCTIONS FOR FINAL FORMATTING

    Option 6, Page Numbering
    Option 1, New Page Number
    Type the number and press Enter
    Press the Escape key three times

C. Search for any new page number codes and delete them:

    F2
    SHIFT + F8
    Option 2, Page
    Option 6, PgNum
    Option 1, New
    Escape
    Back arrow key (to delete)
    Yes (to confirm deletion)

4. Change the footers if desired.

The unmodified Manual Maker files contain a generic footer which labels the pages "Network User's Guide" and places a sequential page number in the outer corner of each page so you can easily copy double-sided pages. If this suits your needs, you needn't change the footers. If you do wish to change the footers, complete these steps.

A. Search for and delete all the old footers.

    First, find and delete the footers on the odd pages:

    F2
    SHIFT + F8

THE NETWARE 286 MANUAL MAKER

       Option 2, Page
       Option 4, Ftr
       Option 1, Footer A
       Escape
       Back arrow key (to delete)
       Yes (to confirm deletion)

Then find and delete the footers on the even pages:

       F2
       SHIFT + F8
       Option 2, Page
       Option 4, Ftr
       Option 2, Footer B
       Escape
       Back arrow key (to delete)
       Yes (to confirm deletion)

B. Create new footers (these instructions tell you how to create the same footer on every page. If you wish to do something more complex, consult the WordPerfect manual).

       SHIFT + F8
       Option 2, Page
       Option 4, Footers
       Option 1, Footer A
       Option 2, Every Page
       Type the footer
       (for automatic, sequential page numbering, type (Control + B)
       Press F7 twice to exit

5. Generate the table of contents and correct page references.

INSTRUCTIONS FOR FINAL FORMATTING

The Manual Maker files contain the codes necessary to generate a table of contents and correct page references. You can do both in the same operation.

A. Go to the very end of the document (HOME, HOME, down arrow key).

B. Define the table of contents:
   ALT + F5
   Option 5, Define
   Option 1, Define Table of Contents
   Option 1, Number of Levels
   Escape (to exit)

C. Generate the table of contents and page references.

   ALT + F5
   Option 6, Generate
   Yes

   NOTE: If you try to print before generating, you will get this message: "Document may need to be generated. Print anyway?" This is because the current table of contents and page references are inaccurate, since they were generated in the previous version of the document.

D. Move the table of contents to the desired position in the document, taking care not to throw the pagination off (insert a New Page Number code if necessary).

6. Select the appropriate printer if necessary:

   SHIFT + F7
   Select Printer

THE NETWARE 286 MANUAL MAKER

> (specify the printer)
> Escape

7. Print hard copy and proofread it to make sure that your manual appears as you wish it to appear. Make any changes that are still necessary.

8. Once you're satisfied, print final hard copy.

9. Make an archive copy of the final manual and store it in a safe place.

10. Xerox as many copies of your manual as you need, bind them as desired, and distribute them to your users.

INSTRUCTIONS FOR FINAL FORMATTING

Formatting Other Types of Files

If you imported the ASCII text included with this book into a word processor or text editor, you will have to do most of your own internal formatting. If you haven't already done this, go ahead and do so now. Then return to this section for general instructions on final formatting.

1. Retrieve all the files into one file.

   Unless your manuals will be very long (100+ pages), I recommend that you make them all one big file. This will make final formatting easier.

   To do so,

   A. Retrieve the first file you wish to include in your manual.

   B. Save the file under a new name—preferably one which describes the manual you're making.

   C. Go to the very end of the file.

   D. Retrieve the second file into this file.

   E. Continue with steps C and D until you have retrieved all the desired files into your manual file. Then save the file again.

2. Delete the Notes to Supervisors.

   I recommend that you create a macro to delete the Notes to Supervisors. I can't tell you the specifics, but generally, the macro should consist of these steps:

   Find the words "Comment Begin"
   Go to the beginning of the word "Comment"

THE NETWARE 286 MANUAL MAKER

> Turn a block on
> Find the words "Comment End" (thus marking the block which is the entire note)
> Delete the block

3. Page through the document and adjust the spacing as desired, eliminating any awkward page breaks, etc.

4. Make sure that the page numbering will be sequential.

5. Create footers if desired.

6. Mark the text for a table of contents and index if desired.

7. Print hard copy and proofread it to make sure that your manual appears as you wish it to appear. Make any changes that are still necessary.

8. Once you're satisfied, print final hard copy.

9. Make an archive copy of the final manual and store it in a safe place.

10. Xerox as many copies of your manual as you need, bind them as desired, and distribute them to your users.

INSTRUCTIONS FOR FINAL FORMATTING

M&T BOOKS

A Library of Technical References from M&T Books

NetWare User's Guide
by Edward Liebing

Endorsed by Novell, this book informs NetWare users of the services and utilities available, and how to effectively put them to use. Contained is a complete task-oriented reference that introduces users to NetWare and guides them through the basics of NetWare menu-driven utilities and command line utilities. Each utility is illustrated, thus providing a visual frame of reference. You will find general information about the utilities, then specific procedures to perform the task in mind. Utilities discussed include NetWare v2.1 through v2.15. For advanced users, a workstation troubleshooting section is included, describing the errors that occur. Two appendixes, describing briefly the services available in each NetWare menu or command line utility are also included.

Book only   **Item #071-0**   **$24.95**

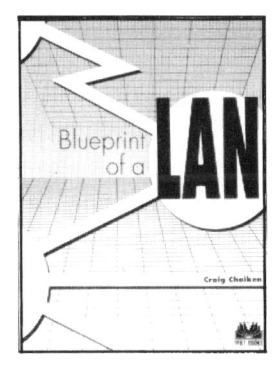

Blueprint of a LAN
by Craig Chaiken

Blueprint of a LAN provides a hands-on introduction to microcomputer networks. For programmers, numerous valuable programming techniques are detailed. Network administrators will learn how to build and install LAN communication cables, configure and troubleshoot network hardware and software, and provide continuing support to users. Included are a very inexpensive zero-slot, star topology network, remote printer and file sharing, remote command execution, electronic mail, parallel processing support, high-level language support, and more. Also contained is the complete Intel 8086 assembly language source code that will help you build an inexpensive to install, local area network. An optional disk containing all source code is available.

Book & Disk (MS-DOS)   **Item #066-4**   **$39.95**
Book only   **Item #052-4**   **$29.95**

M&T BOOKS

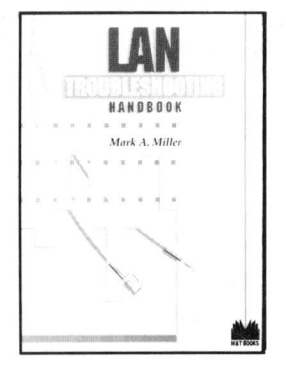

LAN Troubleshooting Handbook
by Mark A. Miller

This book is specifically for users and administrators who need to identify problems and maintain a LAN that is already installed. Topics include LAN standards, the OSI model, network documentation, LAN test equipment, cable system testing, and more. Addressed are specific issues associated with troubleshooting the four most popular LAN architectures: ARCNET, Token Ring, Ethernet, and StarLAN. Each are closely examined to pinpoint the problems unique to its design and the hardware. Handy checklists to assist in solving each architecture's unique network difficulties are also included.

Book & Disk (MS-DOS)	Item #056-7	$39.95
Book only	Item #054-0	$29.95

Building Local Area Networks with Novell's NetWare
by Patrick H. Corrigan and Aisling Guy

From the basic components to complete network installation, here is the practical guide that PC system integrators will need to build and implement PC LANs in this rapidly growing market. The specifics of building and maintaining PC LANs, including hardware configurations, software development, cabling, selection criteria, installation, and on-going management are described in a clear "how-to" manner with numerous illustrations and sample LAN management forms. *Building Local Area Networks* gives particular emphasis to Novell's NetWare, Version 2.1. Additional topics covered include the OS/2 LAN manager, Tops, Banyan VINES, internetworking, host computer gateways, and multisystem networks that link PCs, Apples, and mainframes.

Book & Disk (MS-DOS)	Item #025-7	$39.95
Book only	Item #010-9	$29.95

1-800-533-4372 (in CA 1-800-356-2002)

M&T BOOKS

NetWare Supervisor's Guide
by John T. McCann, Adam T. Ruef, and Steven L. Guengerich

Written for network administrators, consultants, installers, and power users of all versions of NetWare, including NetWare 386. Where other books provide information on using NetWare at a workstation level, this definitive reference focuses on how to administer NetWare. Contained are numerous examples which include understanding and using NetWare's undocumented commands and utilities, implementing system fault tolerant LANs, refining installation parameters to improve network performance, and more.

Book only　　　　　　　　　**Item #111-3**　　　**$24.95**

LAN Protocol Handbook
by Mark A. Miller, P.E.

Requisite reading for all network administrators and software developers needing in-depth knowledge of the internal protocols of the most popular network software. It illustrates the techniques of protocol analysis—the step-by-step process of unraveling LAN software failures. Detailed are how Ethernet, IEEE 802.3, IEEE 802.5, and ARCNET networks transmit frames of information between workstations. From that foundation, it presents LAN performnce measurements, protocol analysis methods, and protocol analyzer products. Individual chapters thoroughly discuss Novell's NetWare, 3Com's 3+ and 3+Open, IBM Token-Ring related protocols, and more!

Book only　　　　　　　　　**Item 099-0**　　　**$34.95**

1-800-533-4372 (in CA 1-800-356-2002)

M&T BOOKS

ORDER FORM

To Order: Return this form with your payment to M&T books, 501 Galveston Drive, Redwood City, CA 94063 or **call toll-free 1-800-533-4372 (in California, call 1-800-356-2002).**

ITEM #	DESCRIPTION	DISK	PRICE

Subtotal _____

CA residents add sales tax ___% _____

Add $3.50 per item for shipping and handling _____

TOTAL _____

Charge my:
- ☐ **Visa**
- ☐ **MasterCard**
- ☐ **AmExpress**

- ☐ **Check enclosed, payable to M&T Books.**

CARD NO. _____

SIGNATURE _____ EXP. DATE _____

NAME _____

ADDRESS _____

CITY _____

STATE _____ ZIP _____

M&T GUARANTEE: If your are not satisfied with your order for any reason, return it to us within 25 days of receipt for a full refund. Note: Refunds on disks apply only when returned with book within guarantee period. Disks damaged in transit or defective will be promptly replaced, but cannot be exchanged for a disk from a different title.

8000